PRAYERS OF SMOKE

Barbara Means Adams

PRAYERS
of SMOKE

Renewing Makaha
Tribal Tradition

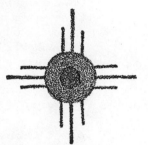

CELESTIAL ARTS
Berkeley, California

CELESTIAL ARTS
P.O. Box 7327
Berkeley, California 94707

Cover design by Ken Scott
Cover concept by Melvin Adams and John Martindale
Author photo by Doug Barnes, *Freedom Socialist*
Text design by Nancy Austin
Composition by Auto-Graphics
Set in Bembo

Library of Congress Cataloging-in-Publication Data

Adams, Barbara Means.
    Prayers of smoke : renewing Makaha tribal tradition / Barbara
Means Adams.
        p.   cm.
    Includes index.
    ISBN 0-89087-567-7
    1. Adams, Barbara Means.   2. Oglala Indians—Biography.
3. Oglala Indians—Religion and mythology.   4. Oglala
Indians—Folklore.   5. Indians of North America—Great
Plains—Biography.   6. Indians of North America—Great
Plains—Religion and mythology.   7. Indians of North
America—Great Plains—Folklore.   I. Title.
E99.03A33   1990
299'.785—dc20   89-7051
                                                                     CIP
First Printing, 1990

0 9 8 7 6 5 4 3 2 1

Manufactured in the United States of America

CONTENTS

ACKNOWLEDGMENTS

My gratitude and thanks to:

My son Melvin, whose vision helped sharpen the focus of my thoughts and revealed the design of the book jacket.

My son Richard, who believed in my ability to finish this book.

My son James, whose love of astronomy was a constant inspiration.

My son Theodore, for providing me with three grandchildren, Justin, Valyssa and Leonard, so that I can experience the joys of being a grandmother and passing my traditions on to yet another generation.

My grandmothers, Theresa and Myrtle, who nursed the book and me through thick and thin. Their understanding and rich heritage were a continual source of renewal for me.

My great-grandmothers, Fannie and Frances (both deceased), whose storytelling enriched my life.

My grandfather Theodore (deceased), who started encouraging me when I was three years old to express myself in writing.

My mother, Margaret, who gave me life and love.

My brothers, Robert, Leonard (deceased), Clayton, Michael, Marvin and Clement, who read the book as it took shape and offered advice all along the way.

My sisters, Theodora, Ramona, Anita and JoAnn, who contributed so much to my research.

My husband, Russel (deceased), whose spirituality enriched my life and who continues to guide me.

My friend Jack for his advice and cover sketches.

My editor, Linda, whose keen eye and high editorial standards helped complete my vision of a book.

My typist, Betty, for her hard work and moral support.

All my friends for their ongoing dedication to the renewal of spirituality.

And all future generations to be inspired by the seven great rituals.

To my grandmother, Theresa Two Two Means

Seven Campfires
(Ooeti Sakowan)

Spider *(Iktome)*

Sky *(Mapiyato)*

1 / THE MAKAHA
SPIRITUAL LANDSCAPE:

A native daughter reclaims it

I am two people. One is an insignificant person, leading the most insignificant of lives. The other is a receiver of the ancient wisdom of the Makaha, a tribe that has much to teach about our place in the universe.

I am a Makaha, the granddaughter of Theresa and Theodore Means. My family is from Wounded Knee, South Dakota, and goes back to the great leader, American Horse.

The Makaha are a sub-band of the Oyuphe band of Little Wound, son of Bull Bear. The Oyuphe band is one of the seven bands of the Oglala. The Oglala are one of the tribes of the Seven Campfires, or Ocheti Shakowin, also known as Sioux.

Before we became the Oyuphe, we were called the Bear People. Bull Bear was our leader. When Bull Bear was killed, his son Little Wound took over and in the late 1800s moved the people to the Pine Ridge Indian Agency.

My people moved to Wounded Knee Creek and became the Makaha, one of seven sub-bands. The Makaha people were led by my grandmother's grandfather. His name was Nupala, which is interpreted today as Two Two. His Christian name was Edward.

As was the tradition, my parents, Bruce Means and Margaret Yellow Thunder, went to Bear Butte, near Sturgis, South Dakota, for the ritual of conception. The Makaha believe that the old volcano at Bear Butte is the source of all souls. A man and a woman go there and stay until the woman is pregnant. My parents went and performed the ritual in the hope that they would capture a good soul for their first child. After I was born, they returned to Bear Butte and put a flat rock in the fork of a tree as an offering of thanksgiving.

My parents had to be away a lot, working. My grandparents raised me from six months. I had a large extended family, so many great-aunts and great-uncles. They all helped teach me the ways they had been taught.

I listened to the heartbeat of my mother before birth, and later I heard the whispering leaves of the cottonwood trees. The stories, songs and gentle drumbeats of my grandparents brought me fully into the world.

Like any child, I could sit for hours watching the sky, seeing faces, animals and monsters as the clouds shifted shapes. As an Indian child, I learned that it is possible to influence the way the clouds move. The Makaha have a ceremony called *heyoka*, in which the chosen person receives power from Mapiyato, spirit of the sky, to dictate where the clouds go. The Great Mystery, the father of all beings, Wakan Tanka, chooses the people who receive such gifts.

My grandparents lived humbly, but I had all I needed. As my grandmother told me stories, I would sketch the characters on the dirt floor. When the story was over, my grandmother would get her broom and sweep away my drawings. The stories stayed in my memory. Many of them were like this one about the Makaha trickster Iktome:

Iktome is a spider. He wears beaded moccasins and brown buckskin leggings with soft fringes. He wears a deerskin jacket with bright-colored beads sewn on it. His hair is long and black and parted in the middle. Each braid, wrapped in red bands, hangs over a small ear and falls to his shoulder. He paints his face with red and yellow, then he draws big black circles around his eyes. His hands are always into mischief.

He would rather set out a snare than go hunting with bow and arrow. When animals are caught in his trap, they provide his meal for the day. He laughs with a wide open mouth. He never stops admiring himself, so friends soon go away.

No one helps Iktome when he is in trouble. No one really loves him.

Iktome lived alone in a cone-shaped wigwam. One day he sat hungry in his wigwam. Suddenly, he rushed out, dragging his blanket. He spread it on the ground and tore up dry grass to toss into the blanket.

After tying all four corners of the blanket into a knot, Iktome slung the light bundle of grass over his shoulder. He snatched up a willow stick and started up walking with a hop and a leap. The bundle bounced from side to side on his back.

He paused for breath on a hilltop. Shading his eyes from the morning sun, he looked along the river bottom and the lowlands. "Aha," he shouted, satisfied with what he saw.

Wild ducks were dancing and feasting in the marshes. With wings spread out, tip to tip, they moved up and down in a large circle around a drum. The singers nodded and blinked their eyes.

Iktome approached, staggering under the weight of his bundle, using his willow cane to keep his feet under him as he wound down the steep path. One old duck called out to him, "Ho, who is there?"

The other ducks still bobbed up and down in the dance and drummed and sang their song. "Ho, Iktome, old fellow, show us what is in your blanket," the old duck called. "Do not hurry off."

"My friend, I must not spoil your dance," Iktome replied. "You would not care to see what is in my blanket. Sing on. Dance on."

"We must see what you carry. We must see what you carry in your blanket," all the ducks began to shout. Their voices were loud in Iktome's ears. Some of the ducks even brushed their wings against the mysterious bundle.

Finally, Iktome said, "My friends, it is only a pack of songs that I carry."

"Oh, let us hear your songs," the ducks all cried.

Iktome said he would sing his songs.

"Hoye. Hoye," cried the delighted ducks.

"Ha," laughed Iktome, tying the four corners of his blanket a little tighter. "I shall sit no more without food."

With great care, Iktome laid down his bundle. He announced, "First, I will build a round straw house. I never sing my songs in the open air."

Soon the straw hut was ready. One by one, the fat ducks waddled in. Iktome stood beside the door smiling. In a strange low voice, he began to hum. All of a sudden his song burst out in a full voice:

> Istokmus wacipo, tuwayatun wanpi kinhan
> Ista nin shashapi kta
> With eyes closed you must dance
> He who opens his eyes
> Forever red eyes shall have.

The ducks shut their eyes very tightly, holding their wings closely as they began to dance. Iktome began to sing louder and faster.

The old duck, Skiska, peeked at Iktome. "Oh, oh. Run, run. Fly out," he began quacking in terror.

There, beside Iktome's bundle of songs, lay half the ducks. Those who were still alive flew out through the door of the hut. They flew high in the sky. One cried out to the others, "Oh, your eyes are red-red."

"Oh, yours are red-red, too," all the others cried.

Back in the hut, Iktome was laughing as he untied his bundle and placed the ducks inside. He then left the little hut for the rains and winds to tear down. He built a large fire outdoors. He planted sticks around the leaping flames, and to each stick he tied a duck. He buried a few ducks to bake under the ashes. He heaped more willows onto the fire. Then he sat down and crossed his legs, keeping his eyes on the roasting ducks. He sniffed impatiently as he listened to his growling belly.

The wind was playing with an old, moaning tree. The tree swayed from side to side, crying in an old man's voice, "Help. I'll break. I'll fall."

Iktome shrugged his shoulders and did not once take his eyes off the roasting ducks. The dripping of amber oil pleased his hungry eyes.

Still, the old tree man called for help.

"Heh. You make my ears ache," shouted Iktome. He arose and looked around. Then he began to climb the tree to find the source of the sad sound. He placed his foot right on the cracked limb without seeing it. As he stepped into the crack, a strong wind rushed by and pressed the limb's torn edges together. Iktome's foot was caught.

"Oh, my foot is crushed," Iktome cried. He pulled and puffed in vain. Through his tears, he saw a pack of wolves roaming beneath the tree.

"Hey, gray wolves," he said, waving to get their

attention. "Don't come here. My foot is caught in this tree limb, and my roasting ducks are getting cold."

"Oh hear the foolish fellow," sneered the leader of the wolves. "He says that he has a duck feast waiting. Let us hurry there for our share."

Iktome watched helplessly from the tree as the wolves ate up his fat ducks. He heard them crack the small, round bones with their strong teeth. He watched them eat the marrow. His foot pained him more and more. The pain shot through his body. "Hin-hin-hin," sobbed Iktome. Real tears washed away the paint on his cheeks.

The wolves began to leave.

"At least you have left my ducks baking under the ashes," Iktome whispered.

"Ho. Po," shouted the wolves. "He whispers that there are more ducks under the ashes."

They pawed out the ducks with such haste that a cloud of ashes rose like gray smoke.

"Hin-hin-hin," moaned Iktome.

Then the strong wind returned. It pulled the tree limb apart, releasing Iktome's foot. It was too late for Iktome. His ducks were all gone. The old tree man resumed his moaning in pain.

Makaha children learn their values from Iktome. He teaches them how not to behave. He also teaches them to listen to nature. Iktome went hungry because he would not pay attention to the voice of the tree.

I used to see trees sway and then hear them moan, and I was sure that every tree had feelings and could express sadness. My parents told me that the Great Spirit, Wakan Tanka, makes trees moan when he wants a child's attention.

I didn't go to school until I was ten. And until my brothers came to live with us, I had no children to play with. I used to play by myself along an old dirt road.

When I was about four, I started seeing a boy along that road. He looked much older, maybe seventeen. He said his name was Elijah Skyman. He liked to tell me stories, traditional tales about Iktome and other animals. He didn't wear Levi's like other people at that time. He was always dressed in dark clothing, and he wore a black cap that kept his face in shadow.

I mentioned him to my grandmother, but she said my family did not know anyone by that name. I saw him all the time until I went to school. Then I didn't see him again.

Soon after Elijah Skyman appeared, another companion came to me. She was a little girl with long black braids. She must have been about four, the same age as I was. When I first looked at her, I thought she seemed very sad and lost, as if she had been left behind. She wore a tiny scarf and a coat that was buttoned all the way up, even though it was summer. She told me her name was Bright Eyes. She talked to me about how hard it was to go away to school. I did not see her after I was forced to go away to school.

I rediscovered both Elijah Skyman and Bright Eyes when I was an adult, living away from the reservation. One day I was in a library on the University of Washington campus in Seattle. I was drawn upstairs to a certain row in the stacks. The feeling that had hold of me is one I've experienced several times in my life; it is the feeling of being pulled, as if by a magnet. This feeling is accompanied by a sensation of increasing warmth.

The heat became intense, focused. I stopped before a shelf of very old books. One of them was shimmering. I pulled it down. It was a collection of 1880s newspaper writings by Indian children from the Haskell Institute in Lawrence, Kansas. Elijah Skyman's byline was atop many of those stories.

Bright Eyes came back to me through a book, too. I was passing a bookstore and, again, I was drawn inside. There I found a book entitled *Bright Eyes*. I rushed home and collected all my change and went back into that store and bought the book. Bright Eyes's name was Susette La Flesche. She lived in the late 1800s. Her mother was an Omaha Indian.

As I read her biography, I began to see similarities between her life and mine. I am a half-breed like her. Her father was half-French and half-Sioux. So was mine. Also she was a writer about Indian issues, as I am. Now I think that the feeling of abandonment that I picked up from the young Bright Eyes who appeared to me came from her sadness over not having finished her work. I think she wanted another life so that she could continue writing about her people.

I was ten when the police came to my grandparents' house and ordered them to send me to school. My life stopped. I was suddenly surrounded by children, but for the first time I was lonely. The children would taunt me about my simple clothes and ask me how Indians got feathers to grow on their heads. When the little blue and red balls started appearing, my life got even more difficult.

These balls, about the size of baseballs, would roll in out of nowhere. They would bounce around my feet. They would scare the other children, who shouted "witchy" over their shoulders as they ran from me.

I now call these little balls entities. I have accepted their playful and intermittent presence. Each one has a different personality. These entities would not leave me alone. They kept trying to tell me something. I had not asked them to come to me, but I accepted them and tried to listen.

I believe that certain people are born with the ability

to see into other worlds, and those worlds will never stop demanding their attention. Sometimes the messengers from those worlds take strange forms.

The teachers at Catholic school dismissed all my traditional beliefs as witchcraft, but they could not convince me to abandon my heritage. In the end, it's all the same god, just different rituals.

As an adult, I began to regain the access to other worlds I had known as a child. I believe that the past, present and future exist simultaneously. Our consciousness moves and selects from among them.

I began to get visions. I had many glimpses of the past tragedies of my people, particularly of the bitter massacre at Wounded Knee in the winter of 1890.

Sometimes my visions are so intense that they upset my normal eating and sleeping patterns for days. My body is under tremendous pressure until the vision has run its course. Sometimes I feel like a puppet, being jerked around. I get weary, even exhausted, as in battle fatigue.

Often, instead of having a vision, I will write for hours, unaware of what I'm writing until I have recovered enough to read it. I can sit with a tablet and pencil and never know that I have lifted that pencil to write until I come out of my trance and am able to read in my own handwriting the information that has been given to me. This also happens when I am sitting at a typewriter. I cross into another world and come back with words typed on paper about what I have found there.

I sometimes receive a vision and do automatic writing at the same time. I remember one such occasion when I felt myself to be floating near the ceiling, laughing and shaking. I looked down and noticed my poor body sitting on the bed. Its hands were scribbling away on a legal pad. I resented the idea that I would have to return to that pitiful body when I was having so much fun floating. I was like a crystal prism; every time I moved, I set rainbows dancing. I was so pretty and having such a great time, and there below was my old body working diligently to write something. It was as if one force was trying to get me out of the way by entertaining me while another used my body to communicate.

When I later read what my body had written, I was shocked and horrified. It was all about my husband's death. This was in April of 1979. He died July 4, 1979. What I had written told me how bad I would feel when he died and advised me that the ritual of the sweat lodge would pull me through.

Much of what I have seen and written has gone into the making of this book. I believe that two beings, first one and then the other, have been prompting me for twenty years to record more of the oral tradition and rituals of the Makaha. The stories my grandparents told me and the ceremonies that led my people along a spiritual path are in danger of being lost.

One of the entities concerned with preserving the stories and rituals is an old woman who wears a striped shawl and a scarf tied on her head. I first saw her when I was in the labor room giving birth to my son James in 1966. There were complications, and I almost died. As I was about to leave this life, the old woman appeared to me and said in Olakota: "You still have a lot of things to do." That brought me back. She has come to me many times since then, taking over my body when I'm sitting at the typewriter. I could not have written this book without her.

The other guiding entity who wants new generations to learn and preserve the old ways is an old man. He has a light in his head, a blue light shining from his forehead. He is tall, about six feet four inches. He knows many things. He is the keeper of knowledge.

He first appeared to me in 1981. He had been trying to get through to me for a whole year. Finally, he contacted a medicine man in Darrington, Washington, a town north of Seattle, where I live. He told the medicine man he was trying to bring me certain gifts, but I wasn't listening. The medicine man, who was not from my tribe, sent word to me. I responded to his request that we hold a ceremony.

The ceremony was January 27, 1981. The entity that was the old man appeared and told me that my power would be the stick. He promised to give me a special understanding. I saw three buckskin bundles, and slowly they faded away.

Three years later, I met a woman at a pow wow. I knew I had to talk to her. We became friends, and later she went to California to go on a retreat with a very old Cherokee man. When she arrived at his lodge, he told her he had seen her come to him in a vision. He said he knew she was the person to take a bundle that had been in his possession for years. She was to deliver the bundle to her friend, Barbara Adams.

She brought the buckskin bundle to me. Inside it was a crystal that changes colors. Sometimes it is coppery. When it is clear, you can see a little limb inside it. That is the stick that is my power.

I have yet to receive the second and third bundles that I saw.

The old Cherokee man received the bundle when he was thirty-three and held it in safekeeping for me for sixty-three years. When he died in September of 1987, he was ninety-nine years old. I have had communication with him since his death. I never met him while he was alive.

After I had had the crystal for awhile, a friend had a vision about it. He told me that the crystal was part of a staff that was held by a leader about 4000 B.C. All over the world, people have parts of this staff. Some day, all these people will come together.

The crystal gave me more of an insight into what I am supposed to do. It gave me the power to complete this book, to record the creation stories of my people, to re-discover the source of our beliefs and rituals. I am grateful for the power to receive these things and to put them back out into the world.

Much of my gratitude is for the chance to leave something to my four sons. They are all searching for ways to live in the world. They are torn between the dominant white culture and the Makaha traditions I have tried to keep alive for them. The pressures on them to conform to white ways are tremendous. When I was a child, I could sit by a cottonwood tree and hear the wisdom it whispered. My boys have grown up alongside telephone poles instead.

My hope is that the stories here will remind them of their tie to the past and stir that part of them that longs for the land of their ancestors. That land can still be theirs, in spirit. It can be a spiritual home to anyone who would keep the words and ways that sustain it.

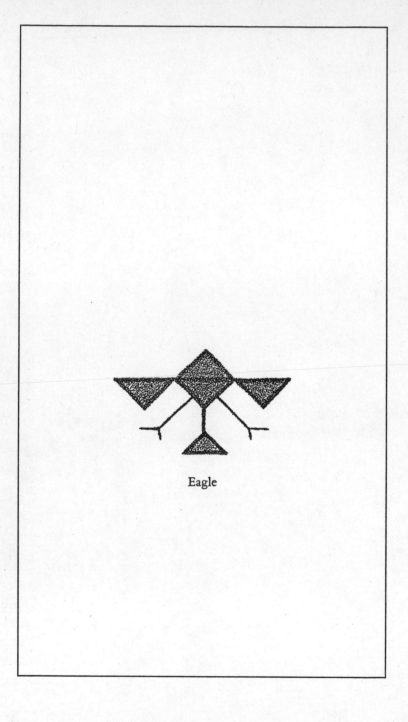

Eagle

2 / FOUR PARTS OF THE SOUL:

Eye, breath, animal twin and guardian come together

As a child, I knew there were four parts of the soul. No one could tell me what they were. No one remembered. Eventually, I learned the names of the four parts. The guiding entities of this book helped me understand them.

The soul is called *sicun*. It enters the embryo at the time of conception. It contains three of the beings: *tonwan*, *niya* and *chekpa*. The fourth being, *nagi*, protects the other three and makes sure *sicun* lives on after the body is gone.

The first being is *tonwan*, the eye, who sees everything. *Tonwan* can leave the body. In infants, *tonwan* has an easy exit through the soft spot on their heads.

My *tonwan* comes and goes frequently through the top of my head. It causes an unbearable tension as it leaves. My head feels as if it is going to burst. When *tonwan* returns, I feel only a little heat unless *tonwan* wants to make an impression. One time, my *tonwan* moved like lightning from the ceiling back into my head. The tips of my fingers and toes burned. My whole body quivered at the shock, and I passed out for a few minutes.

Indian people never touch or strike the top of the head. The Makaha people cut the scalp or a lock of the hair above the forehead because we believe that the skin and hair there cover the *tonwan* and are sacred. Long ago, the warrior took a small scalp from the enemy and purified it in smoke so that the four parts of the victim's soul would travel peacefully to the other world.

No one ever steps over the head of a sleeping child or adult. If hair is lying on the floor, it is immediately picked up so that no one will step over it. If someone does step over a person's head or hair lying on the floor, we have a ceremony so that nothing bad will happen.

Most Indian people do not like to live in houses of two or more stories because if they did, they would be constantly walking on top of each other's beings.

The energy of *tonwan* turns to a turquoise blue as it leaves the body. My youngest son Melvin and I watched that beautiful light leave my niece's body four days after her death. We always wait four days before we bury our loved ones.

One evening I was sitting on my bed when I felt *tonwan*'s restlessness. Suddenly, I was a brilliant gold snakelike flash of light. Then I was an eye, looking up, down, north, south, east and west all at once. Then I was several hundred prisms. I knew what it was like to be in the eternal present.

Later, when I was looking at drawings of atoms in a science text, I suddenly knew what that golden snake and those hundreds of prisms meant. *Tonwan* was the atom. Or the atom was *tonwan*.

The Greek philosopher Democritus said that the soul

is composed of the finest, roundest, most nimble and fiery of atoms—a perfect description of *tonwan*.

A nineteenth century German chemist, Friedrich August Kekule von Stradonitz, had a vision similar to mine. He described sitting in front of a fire and sinking into reverie. He saw atoms dancing and coming together to form long chains. The chains snaked about. Then one of the snakes caught its own tail and whirled before the chemist's eyes. This image gave him the hexagonal form of the benzene molecule.

My vision gave me the form of one part of *sicun*. When it changed from a snake into an eye of a hundred prisms, I tried very hard to maintain that level.

I told my grandmother about my vision. She said that the eye symbolized the eye of the spotted eagle. "It is our *tonwan*, the eye," she said, "that poises like an eagle, always ready to fly in any direction to capture an attractive idea or event, then to bring it back to the physical body as a trophy of vision."

Grandfather Black Elk said: "It was the pictures I remembered and the words that went along with them; for nothing I have ever seen with my eyes was so clear and bright as what my vision showed me; and no words that I have ever heard with my ears were like the words I heard."

I have seen other manifestations of the eyes of *tonwan*. On October 18, 1980, I was awakened by a bright light in my face. The light came in through the west window. I tried to see its source, but as I got closer, I began to burn. I had to pull my window shade down. Sweat was pouring from my body, and the light was still coming through.

My desire to see what was out there was stronger than my fear of burning. I raised the shade and ran back to where I could stand to look again. I saw that the light had coalesced into a gigantic wheel. As it swirled, it cast rays. Each ray had an eye on it. There must have been a million eyes. The wheel grew to a forty-foot diameter, flinging eyes all around it.

Although Indian people knew the form of the wheel, they did not believe in putting it to work for such an ordinary thing as physical transportation. They knew the wheel had eyes to bring them visions, and they used it in ceremonies. Today these wheels are called medicine wheels.

Visions are different from dreams. A vision can occur during sleep, but the jolt of *tonwan*'s leaving and returning disturbs. When *tonwan* leaves, the body feels a slight chill. When *tonwan* returns, the body feels heat.

Tonwan tends to wander all the time. The roaming *tonwan* has to pay attention to certain landmarks or else it may never find its way back to the body. This need to fix points along its journey is why we can recognize certain places even though we have never been there before. Our *tonwan* has been there, and that house, that tree, that bend in the road were *tonwan*'s reminders of the way back.

Sometimes *tonwan*'s strings to the body are too strong, and it can't go anywhere without dragging the body along. An unfettered *tonwan* can enter into the body of another person or animal. The physical body is like a shell. *Tonwan* uses these shells as hiding places or as forms for communication. Often *tonwan* can get its message across by appearing in the form of an animal.

When *tonwan* leaves while its body is asleep, it can encounter danger. It may be detained on its journey. One *tonwan* can meet another, and they may fight, as in this Makaha story:

The warrior met his foe in the valley called Makaha. The warrior had come out of the dark forest into a dazzle of sunset. His arms were full of sticks. He was in the shadows just where Makaha Valley becomes two valleys, and he was trying to adjust to the brightness beyond.

The valley was noisy. A flock of birds flew by, eyeing him and mocking each other. A large ant pattered past under a load of grass three times bigger than it was. A field mouse swerved, screaming, past the large ant and toward the dark shade of a tree.

A skeleton had been standing near the old tree. At the scream of the mouse, it glanced up and stepped quickly away. The Makaha warrior saw the skeleton and felt a queer jerk of his heart. He immediately looked away. He built a fire and roasted a rabbit for his dinner.

When night had fallen, the skeleton challenged the warrior to a wrestling match. The warrior's fire was very bright and kept him strong. When the fire started to cool, the skeleton grew strong. With all of his will and effort, the warrior used the strength he had left to pull the skeleton into his dying fire. The warrior had won.

During the week before the full moon *tonwan* is most active. I never plan to do much during this time except to burn sage, sweet grass and cedar. This helps me to keep a hold on my *tonwan*.

The second being of the soul is *niya*, the breath.

Niya flies to the mouth of the newborn. This is why childbirth is such a crucial event and only certain women are allowed to help in the delivery of babies. Great precautions must be taken so that *niya* stays with the infant. Everyone keeps her mouth tightly shut until the newborn takes that first breath. Some people even tie the mouths of their animals shut or cover them. If *niya* leaves the baby, and another creature swallows it, the child will die.

During illness, the *niya* being can take flight very easily. It is customary among my people to go and sit with a sick friend or relative. Sometimes healing ceremonies are conducted away from the ill person.

The man who does the healing ceremony sends one of his helping spirits to visit and to examine the sick person. The helping spirit pats the sick person's body before it leaves to return to the healer. Sometimes the helping spirit is gone for several hours.

I have felt the healing helpers. On May 26, 1981, I was to have an operation. The night before, I was awakened by a gentle pat. I opened my eyes but could not see anyone. The gentle patting continued.

Later, I learned that my mother was having a healing ceremony for me at the time.

The next day, during my operation, my *tonwan* left my body and was floating above. It was the size of a baseball. I could hear people talking in the operating room. I could watch as they worked on my lungs and then closed the incision with metal clips.

Suddenly, my *tonwan* felt a strange coldness and began to drift away from my body. It felt as if it were in a swiftly flowing river, trying to swim upstream.

I could hear the excited voices of the medical team. They were saying that my blood pressure was dropping, and that I needed oxygen. *Niya* was leaving. *Tonwan* was shrinking to the size of a quarter.

Niya did not escape entirely, and I survived. However, I suffered from a strange coldness that would not leave me. It seemed I was chilled to the marrow all the time. I would sit by a fire until my skin began to turn red. Still, I would feel as if I were trapped in a gray, cold bubble.

In February a medicine man worked with me for a whole night. He used a huge cedar board with a hole at the bottom where four people could hang on. The board became so powerful that it lifted the four men off the floor. Like a bird, it swooped and swept the men off their feet. Then the board would swoop in and touch me, trying to lift the bubble of cold that surrounded me. Finally, the board pierced the bubble and removed it. By early morning, I felt warm and whole once again.

Indian people believe that *niya* leaves through the mouth at the time of death. This is the reason we never strike another person in the face.

I watched the *niya* being slowly leave my husband Russel Adams. On July 1, 1979, around 3:30 A.M., he got up and went into the kitchen for a glass of water. I heard the glass shatter, and he called my name. When I got to him, his face was white and he was staring at the shards of glass in his hand.

Then he said to me: "It's only a matter of time now." He told me how the *niya* being had begun to leave him when he lifted his glass to his lips to take a drink.

All of his *niya* was gone at around 8 P.M. on July 4. His last words were: "Let me rest now."

The third part of the soul is *chekpa*. This being enters the placenta during the mother's pregnancy. When the child is born, the parents make the placenta into a bundle and tie it to the highest branch of a tree. Eventually, a bird or an animal will eat of that placenta and will then carry around the twin of that child's *chekpa* being.

So that the baby can stay in contact with its *chekpa*, the navel string is dried and put in a pouch attached to the shirt or dress of the little one. The pouch is shaped like a turtle. My grandmother says that people who wander constantly from place to place have lost the little pouch containing their navel string. They have lost contact with their *chekpa* being.

Hunters always apologize to the spirits of birds and

animals because they may be carrying someone's *chekpa*. Often killing the bird or animal can cause illness in the person whose *chekpa* they carry. Sometimes the bird or animal spirit of the *chekpa* comes to be by the side of the person who is sick or dying.

Chekpa means twin and is both male and female. The animal or bird spirit that appears to a vision seeker is one who carries the *chekpa* being. The vision seeker knows to treat that animal or bird as an adviser. The *chekpa*'s reflection shows in its blood.

Our Oglala-Oyuphe leader, Crazy Horse, looked into the blood of an owl to see his *chekpa*'s reflection. He was preparing for battle. After seeing the reflection, he removed his *tonwan* from his body. Thus he became invincible in combat.

He followed this ritual every time he prepared for battle, including the time he met General Custer at the Little Bighorn River in Dakota Territory in June of 1876.

My grandmother still tells a story about Crazy Horse and his medicine bundle. My people make medicine bundles after a vision. We use the fur or feathers of the animal that has appeared to us. We want to capture the spirit of that animal and carry it with us.

Crazy Horse's medicine bundle was about the size of a bedroll. His power was that of the owl, so I assume that owl feathers were part of his medicine bundle. Before he died in September of 1876, he gave the medicine bundle to Jenny Wounded Horse and her husband, Louis Fast Thunder. Jenny was related to Crazy Horse. Jenny and Louis are the great-grandparents of my grandfather, Theodore Means.

Jenny kept the medicine bundle until her death in 1932. Then another relative, Nellie Ghost Dog, became its keeper. No one outside the family ever knew about it.

My grandfather was the next to have responsibility for it after Nellie.

During World War II, when my grandfather was leaving for the U.S. Army, the family decided to bury the medicine bundle. He did not know whether he would come back from the fighting, and he did not want Crazy Horse's medicine bundle to fall into the wrong hands. Everyone was in Minatare, Nebraska, because it was the season to pick corn and potatoes. They selected a burial site and pitched a tent beside it. They dug a six-foot-deep hole. Before putting the medicine bundle in the hole, they decided to unwrap it to see what was in it.

They kept it inside the tent. First they unwrapped the blanket, then several pieces of cloth. They got as far as the small part, which was a buckskin pouch. Before they could open it, scores of owls surrounded the tent. Their wingbeats sounded like thunder. My family wrapped the medicine bundle up and buried it right away.

I have had two experiences with my *chekpa* being. The first occurred in March of 1965 in Pine Ridge, South Dakota, during a terrible, sudden snow storm. This was when my son James was born and I nearly died. I have mentioned that this traumatic time was when I first saw the old woman who is one of the guiding entities of this book. After she appeared to me, I had to go back to the hospital, in relapse two weeks after my first recovery. I was lying in my hospital room, very weak. Suddenly, a small gray bird came flying through the window. The snow blew in as if there were no glass on the window. Several more birds came and sat on the window ledge. The wind was fluffing up their feathers. Their chirping made me extremely happy.

The first bird sat on the arm of a chair near my bed. It seemed to be waiting for something to happen. When it flew back to the ledge and, with the others, into the snowstorm, I knew I would survive.

My second experience with my *chekpa* being came in January of 1981. I was not feeling well, so I had an Indian healer come to me. During the healing ceremony, the small gray bird appeared to him. It was trying to pick up a flat stone that was too big for it to carry. I'm not sure what the bird's activity symbolized, but I felt better after it appeared to the medicine man.

The fourth and last part of the soul is *nagi*, the guardian. *Nagi* never enters the body but is nearby at all times. *Nagi* brings warnings. It appears to relatives and friends before its body dies or is hurt. *Nagi* is sometimes in human form for these appearances.

Most of the time, *nagi* is lamenting. The thirty-seven tribes of the Plains Indians have a strong belief that if *nagi* takes the form of an owl and hoots three times, someone will die. In fact, there will be three deaths in a family within a year. If *nagi* takes the form of a dog and emits a mournful cry for no apparent reason, that is another warning of death.

An old grandmother once told me of her experience with a *nagi*. She had a buffalo skull in her living room. Her grandson had left it there. One night, the grandmother felt some eyes staring at her. She looked around and was startled to see bright blue eyes staring from the buffalo skull. She turned off the lights and burned sage and sweet grass. The eyes glowed in the dark. The *nagi* did not go away until dawn. A few months later her only son passed away.

Nagi is nothing to be afraid of. It prepares a person for an accident or death.

Nagi can be very noisy. It laughs, sneezes, coughs, hums, whistles, snores, sings and cries. It has a loud walk

and an even heavier running gait. Sometimes *nagi* knocks
on walls, windows or doors. Sometimes *nagi* reaches out
and touches.

Once when I was thirteen, I was lying on a bed in a
tent. It was summer, so I didn't have any shoes on. I was
dangling my feet over the side of the bed while I read a
comic book.

I felt hands touching my toes. I turned around to yell
at my pesky cousin Doris. I didn't see Doris.

I sat up. Then hands touched my ankles and legs.
Those hands were icy cold. They began pulling on my
feet. I still could see no one, but I felt a strong pulling. I
started to scream.

When my parents came in, they found nothing. It
was probably the *nagi* of my grandfather, Edward Black
Bear, who had died earlier that evening. *Nagi* tries very
hard to get children to follow it. This is the reason that
my people watch very carefully over small children for a
year or two after someone dies. *Nagi* has trouble hypno-
tizing a child if an adult is around.

Nagi's face is always hidden, either by a hood, a hat
or long hair. Usually, *nagi* will not look a person in the
face.

Several times I have seen beings that I recognized as
*Nagi*s. They laugh and talk among themselves as we do.

Once, I was boarding a bus to go back home after a
visit to my grandparents in Wounded Knee. I heard a
voice telling me to take a good look at my grandfather.
"This will be the last time you ever see him alive," the
voice warned. I sat down in my seat and stared out the
window at my grandfather, who stood below me waving
good-bye. I tried hard to memorize every line on his face.
Five weeks later, I got a call informing me of his death.

The *nagi* of my brother Leonard Means brought me

a message in March of 1970. Leonard was living with me then. He had asked to borrow my car so that he could go to town.

Next thing I knew, my brother was at the front door calling to me. It was 2 A.M. I unlocked the door and let him in. I told him there was a roast in the oven and freshly baked bread on the counter. He went into the kitchen and started making coffee. He was very noisy and talked to me about the girl he had met that night.

He also told me that he had taken a long drive with a friend of his and that the car had stalled twenty miles from home. His friend had stayed in the car. He said he wanted to take some coffee and sandwiches to him. He asked me for ten dollars to help with towing expenses.

I put the ten dollars on his dresser and went back to bed. As I was walking back to my room, I noticed that he turned off the kitchen lights and went into his room.

I lay down, and it occurred to me that I should ask my neighbor to drive him back to the car since it was so far away. I was very groggy and not making much sense out of my brother's being there.

I raced to the door to tell Leonard to wake the neighbor and get a ride. He was nowhere in sight. I ran down the block after him, but I couldn't find him.

When I went into the kitchen, I noticed that the roast had not been touched and neither had the bread. The coffee pot was in the sink, as if it had never been used.

I went into my brother's room. The ten-dollar bill was not on the dresser.

Early the next morning, I got a call from the police. They told me that Leonard had been in an accident at 1:45 A.M., about twenty miles west of town. No one found him until 6 A.M. He was unconscious.

When I took his clothes from the hospital to wash them, I found a ten-dollar bill wadded up in one pocket.

When my brother was able to talk a few weeks later, he told me he had been out with a girl that evening. However, he said he had not been home afterwards. And he was not aware of having any money, other than a few coins, in his pocket after his date.

When the *nagi* appears in human form, it is the exact image of the person whose soul it is protecting. Sometimes I don't know whether I'm dealing with the person or the *nagi*. Many times I have seen a person pass through a room with his twin tagging along behind him. My two cats keep their *nagis* close by, too. Some nights I open my window four times to let in the two cats and their *nagis*.

One night in September of 1982, my son Melvin came into my bedroom. I had been sleeping, but his footsteps awakened me. Before I could say anything, he walked back out into the living room.

I called to him and asked whether anything was wrong. He told me that he had seen a man with long hair sitting in my room looking out the window. We burned sage and sweet grass all the rest of the night for the wandering *nagi*.

Several days later, when my oldest son Theodore brought his senior class portraits home, I found that one of them was of Leonard. That shock was another warning.

My brother was then living in South Dakota. A letter from him arrived soon after I saw his profile among Theodore's pictures. He wanted to come to live with me again in Snohomish, Washington, he said. I went to South Dakota to pick him up and take him to my home.

In November, he was home alone when knocking on the bedroom door, lights going on and off and footsteps kept him awake all night.

The next night, he was still alone. He decided to move downstairs into the room where we kept the ceremonial pipe. He heard voices in the kitchen. Carrying sage for protection, Leonard crept to the kitchen door. The light was on. In the kitchen he saw several men, all with their backs to him. One turned to look at him. He froze because the one looking at him was his twin.

In December, my brother moved from my house. I didn't hear from him for a long time.

At 2 A.M. on February 10, I was awakened by flashing lights. I went out onto my deck to watch them. They flashed over a lake that the Indians of the Northwest called Flowing Lake, the Trail of the Spirits. I stood and prayed for all the people who were dying at that hour. I felt such loneliness that I cried.

On the afternoon of February 17, I got a call from the county morgue. Leonard's body had been there since February 10.

He had been shot coming out of a convenience store. The man who shot him, we learned later, had announced to other tenants in his apartment building that he was going out to kill somebody, anybody, that night.

My mother told me later that the night before my brother was killed, she heard an owl hoot three times outside her home in South Dakota. That night, also, several men dressed in cowboy outfits entered the room in my mother's house where my uncle slept. The three men appeared three times to my uncle. The third time, he recognized one of them as Leonard.

My brother's *nagi* wandered most of his life.

I get easily hypnotized by the *nagi* beings. When I was a child, I followed the *nagi* of a grandfather who had died. I was afraid to have him see me, so I hid behind a tree every time the *nagi* stopped to look at something. The grandfather's *nagi* was young. As it walked along the tree line, the *nagi* came to a hill. I heard laughter from the other side of the hill. I saw the grandfather's dead relatives greet him and take him away. I was afraid to follow.

A person's *nagi* will show up in water and in mirrors. When a person is sick, he never looks in a mirror. He is faced away from the window, or it is covered.

Portraits reflect the *nagi*. They are used in ceremonies when people are lost, sick or believed to be dead. When a neighbor boy was run over by a van and lying unconscious in the hospital, I saw his *nagi* outside the house for several nights. I asked a medicine man to hold a healing ceremony. We gathered at sunrise and used a portrait of the boy. His whole family came. A friend stayed with him in the hospital. That friend reported that at 5 A.M. she felt such a strong force come into the hospital room that she left and stood by the door. A few hours later, the boy opened his eyes for the first time in two weeks. He recovered fully, amazing all the doctors.

Dawn (*Anpetu*):
Darkness and light were two warriors
who kept arguing. They chased each
other around the world. Dawn is
between them to keep them apart.

Souls Waiting to Be Born
(*Hoksicalapi*)

Water, Thunder Being:
the second element
(*Wakinyan, Heyoka* ceremony)

Four Winds or
the Four Directions:
Yata, the north wind, magpie;
Eya, the west wind;
Yanpa, the south wind, owl;
Okaga, the east wind, meadowlark

Creator
(also *Peta Yuhala*)

3 / CREATION STORIES FROM THE FIRST WORLD:

The universe settles into seven sacred circles

Because I knew very early that I was different and that other worlds intruded on my consciousness no matter how hard I tried to ignore them, I looked for ways to understand what was happening to me.

An old medicine man known as Fools Crow, of Kyle, South Dakota, gave me a very good piece of advice. What he told me was: "Anything you want to know, study the sky."

I got a simple book on the stars that became like a prayer book for me. I would take it out on clear nights, and I would study the sky. It was a kind of meditation.

I began to realize how close to nature we are. This is something my ancestors knew. My generation, though, is forgetting the old wisdom.

My ancestors had seven great rituals to celebrate our connection to the universe and to one another. I began to seek out the people who still observe those rituals and to get much more involved.

I was not satisfied with just going through the motions and the prayers and the chants. I wanted to know where the rituals came from, what originally gave them meaning.

I did research everywhere I could think of. I went to museums and archives and read everything I could find about the American Indian. I was searching for a connection. I felt something was missing in everything I read.

The Sacred Pipe, which is Black Elk's account of the seven great rituals, recorded by Joseph Epes Brown, came the closest to revealing the ancient powers. I felt it had some of the truths in it, more than any other source. Still, I knew my search was not over.

One day, to my surprise, I found what I was looking for in a sheaf of papers that I had begun collecting when I was five years old. These were what I call creation stories, simple tales about the origin of everything. My great-great-grandmother, Fanny Fast Thunder Means, had told them to me at bedtime. So had my grandfather, Theodore Means, and my grandmother, Theresa Means. As soon as I was old enough, I began to write them down.

The creation stories are part of the rich Makaha oral tradition. The events they recount happened "a long time ago." To a child, "a long time ago" might as well be the day before yesterday. As my grandmother told me about how the sun found its place in the sky and how the moon got its phases, I felt close to those occurrences and was ready at any moment to witness new episodes of similar cosmic magnitude.

I wrote the stories in both English and Olakota. My grandfather taught me to read and write. I tied the pages together with yarn.

When I went away to Catholic school, I took my little yarn-knotted books with me. The nuns decided they could keep me occupied by teaching me how to type. I used the creation stories to practice. I transferred them from a child's painstaking lettering to typescript. The nuns paid no attention to what I was typing. They complimented me on my increasing proficiency.

My rediscovery of these childhood stories as the source of the seven great rituals and all the powerful symbolism of my people was not the end of my search. In many ways, it was only the beginning. I had a mass of material, more than a thousand stories. I had only a dim understanding and no organizing principle.

Then the two guiding entities of this book became active. My work with them was the most intense during sixteen months beginning in July of 1981. I typed and retyped day and night. I seemed to be possessed first by the old woman and then by the old man. I was typing and retyping the stories I had known by heart since I was a child, but for the first time an understanding of what they meant and the power they contained began to seep through.

The Makaha creation stories are all centered in the area of the United States around the Black Hills. Many of the basic concepts of the stories are the same as those in the creation stories of other tribes. Only the details differ according to quirks of local geology.

With the guidance of the old man and the old woman, I have organized the stories according to the four ages or worlds that make up a cycle, according to the tradition of my people. The first age is the rock age. The second is the fire age. The third is the bow age. And the fourth is the pipe age. As a cycle moves through the ages, things of a spiritual nature are increasingly obscured. We believe that we are currently living in the fourth age, or pipe age, and that soon all will be swept away so the spiritual can resurface and the cycle can begin again.

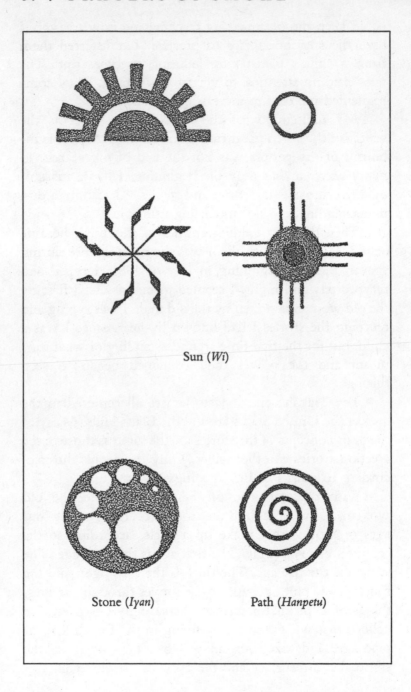

Sun (*Wi*)

Stone (*Iyan*)   Path (*Hanpetu*)

These four divisions of the Makaha creation stories also correspond to the four elements, earth, fire, water and air.

The stories from the first world, which follow here, begin at the beginning, the big bang that created the universe. They all correspond to some celestial event.

The stories move through the events that gave us the seven sacred circles. The circle is our most powerful symbol. And seven is one of our most important numbers.

These traditional creation stories once belonged to a whole people who knew without lengthy explanation that, for instance, the Star Council People are all the heavenly bodies created when Peta Yuhala dropped the giant fireball. Many of the stories that follow may not be immediately clear to those outside the oral tradition of the Makaha people. Time spent in trying to understand them will be amply rewarded. And if something refuses to give up its meaning, remember the advice of Fools Crow: "Study the sky."

STORIES FROM THE FIRST WORLD

The first sacred circle is the spinning of everything in the universe after the pieces blow apart. The celestial events correspond to the current-day big-bang theory of creation of the universe.

There is an old knowledge of Peta Yuhala, the fire carrier, who organized the First Council of Stars—*Wichahpi Omnichye.*

He owned a bundle of four powers.

The first power caused the wind to move and changed the four seasons yearly.

The second power burned the skin.

The third power made the plants grow.

The fourth power was heat.

Peta Yuhala, the fire carrier, used his powers to make a fireball. He took so long in making the fireball that it became gigantic and heavy. When Peta Yuhala lifted the ball on his back, he staggered and fell.

The fireball bounced far, far away, breaking into many pieces.

The part of the ball that was left, Peta Yuhala gathered up and put back into his creation bundle.

Peta Yuhala took the last piece of the fireball from his bundle and called it Iyan or Tunka, the Stone.

Only Iyan could name things.

Suddenly, Iyan was surrounded by an intense form of darkness. This dense murk was Hanpetu, the beautiful spirit of fertility.

Iyan could feel the warm blood running in his veins. The waters emerged from his blue blood. Mists rolled over Iyan, the very first breath. Mists carried the blue up to form the sky. Iyan named the sky Mapiyato and told him to be judge over all.

Mapiyato shook and breathed fire.

Iyan felt sweat drip down his back, tumbling, tumbling away like berries. Slowly, Iyan began to crumble until he became a tiny pebble. He continued to perspire as the rest of him became earth. Iyan named his earth daughter Maka.

Maka's image was in the clouds. The clouds molded her a round face. Her bones were made of fine star dust. She was bluish-white and fragile.

Iyan gave her a drum for a heart. The drumbeat became her heartbeat. The drum beat, and life began.

Maka soon became a beautiful woman. She drifted endlessly in the darkness that was Hanpetu. Maka wanted light. She asked that Hanpetu be banished to the bottom of the cold world.

Mapiyato sent Hanpetu far away, thus creating the first sacred circle, which became her path forever.

The second sacred circle is the earth moving around the sun.

Maka wept. She was naked and hungry. She was cold and tired. Mapiyato, so young and handsome, listened quietly to her. He reached out, brushed her cheek, then touched Iyan.

From this new union came a star.

Iyan named the star Wi.

The burning star, so luminous, moved high in the boundless dome, alone, unlimited.

Slowly, Maka trailed her robes of sun rays along the path. She circled the burning star. Once every twelve-moon, she created and kept the second sacred circle.

The third sacred circle is the shape of the earth.

Wi slowly bathed Maka's body in sunlight, breaking through her crevices in long streaks. The sunlight, mixed with Maka's powers, created another spirit, the powerful, winged Wakinyan.

He emerged from the hot, seething, black clouds. His voice was thunder. His eyes were lightning.

Wakinyan's glance was like a frightened snake striking downward, then upward in a frenzy.

Wakinyan brought with him the first war spear and stone ax.

Maka hummed to the drumbeats. From her throat came many honor songs. From her tiny feet came the round dance.

Wi loved to watch her dance and move. Maka danced so hard, turning and turning, that she lost some of her pretty fringes. Everyone looked for them, but they were gone.

This was the third sacred circle.

The fourth sacred circle is the spinning of the earth on its axis.

The spirit of fertility, Hanpetu, became the beautiful wife of Wi. He had given her a soft light. So she became the luminous moon, a shining reflection of the sun. Her name changed to Hanhepi Wi, meaning "the night's burning sun."

At each sunrise, Wi painted a red line on the top of his wife's head, indicating that she was a good woman who never quarreled and bore many children. He put a string of shells around her neck.

In Hanpetu's place, Mapiyato mixed green into yellow, then into red colors, creating Anpo, who broke apart and died after creeping up the eastern sky.

Maka mourned for Anpo.

Mapiyato searched for Anpo. He gazed all over his blue dome. He found her in the twilight. He brought her back, giving her the task of waking up the sun at dawn and the moon at twilight. To this day, Anpo follows her path around and around the universe, creating the fourth sacred circle.

The fifth sacred circle is the rotation of stars around Polaris.

From the mysterious aura of Iyan and Wakinyan, Ksa, the spider spirit of wisdom, came to be. He spoke many languages.

The Star Council had many feasts. Ksa was always invited as a special guest. He was so young and handsome that the people of the Star Council could not take their eyes from him, that charming, dazzling spider-man.

One day, during the council meeting, Ksa was chosen to bring about new living things. He returned to his father's home on top of the highest peak in the cold mountains to plan, to think, to draw, to cut out pieces.

Wakinyan listened very carefully to his son. He asked Hanhepi Wi to help him. They made separate parts for all the plants. For some of the plants, they made the roots; for others, long and short stems or leaves. They made some of the seeds into grains and some into nuts with hard brown shells.

"Are you finished?" Wakinyan asked.

"No," said his son, "we have too many seeds."

"I'll bury all these extra seeds," Wakinyan said.

So they sprinkled seeds of every plant and tree in the meadows, by the beautiful lakes. The buried seeds slept underneath the warm earth. Wi pressed his chest against their bodies and beamed a faithful smile on them and cried: "Oh green grass! Oh green grass!"

Tender shoots grew in the snow. Stems scattered here and there, in silence. There, over there, with delicate breath was a glitter of insects. Things of the earth were everywhere!

The Chekpa Hoksicalapi were the first twin babies, who descended on the silky threads of Ksa's spider web to the mouth of Maka's vagina in the moonlight. The twins had found many plants which they braided and tied together to make a rope on which they would descend into the womb.

Day after day, the Chekpa babies struggled on their braided rope. Finally, they climbed to the place under the navel. There the twins sketched eyes, noses, mouths, bodies, legs, heads and ears. The first creatures arose slowly from the ooze of Maka's womb.

Maka passed on the drum of creation so that the creatures could have heartbeats. Many new creations tried to climb the braided rope out from beneath the navel. The twins returned with the first creation that succeeded in inching along the walls of the vagina, which was like a valley in the twilight. This was the first journey of love.

The Olakota word for love is *tehila.*

The very first creature that emerged from the earthen womb of Maka was named Unktehila, a creature with legs modified into paddles. She became the first water creature. She liked to eat the white meat of the dog. She painted her face red. Her symbol was a plume of down.

The second creature was Uncegila. He was the first male dinosaur. He and Unktehila danced the *wacipipi wakan*, the holy dance of the stars. Their helpers were lizard, snake, owl and eagle.

One day Mapiyato came to Hanhepi Wi and said: "The earth-woman is unhappy and cries. She travels in the dark shadows and whispers your name, hoping that you will return and be her friend."

The other voice was loving and gentle.

"My brother," she said, "you have driven me away from all my people and Maka."

"No, my sister, you must return with all your powers of fertility and birth."

Hanhepi Wi now returns every lunar month.

She returns to the sky-world, her home, where she sits and looks down on us through the nights as the moon and the mother of the first cedar tree.

By and by, Mapiyato had a son, motion. Iyan named him Tate.

His power came from the sage plant.

Unktehila and Uncegila had four sons. Their bodies were scaly, like those of their parents. Ebom, the first-born, was very vicious and became the strongest wind in the sky. Iya, the second-born, was invisible, with a large mouth that swallowed everything when he yawned or when he was hungry. He was known in the universe as the camp eater because when the Star Council People came near him, they swirled in and in, faster and faster, like water running to a plug hole.

Iya, the notorious camp eater, was afraid of the sound of drumbeats, so he never bothered Maka at all. Her heartbeats are very loud.

The third son was Ksapela. He could kill people with his glance, or by capturing their reflection in water. He could appear as a buck or a doe. When he hypnotized innocent people, the children born were part human. They could change into a deer like their father.

He was the founder of the Black Tail Deer Society. (The society no longer has any members; the last ones died three generations ago. People tended to be afraid of the Black Tail Deer Society because the vision of the black-tailed deer conferred the power of hypnosis.)

Mini Watutkala was the fourth son. He was a tiny virus that caused sickness. Two of the Star Council leaders died, one very old and one young and strong. Their bodies were wrapped and placed high on *cowahe*, a scaffold, so they could be near living Star Council People.

Seven big stars were attached to a gigantic staff in the sky. It was here that the old man was buried. Seven little stars were attached to a staff. This became the burial place of the younger one. These two scaffolds still circle Polaris.

This is the fifth sacred circle.

The sixth sacred circle is the movement of the four winds around the earth. It is during the creation of this circle that evil appears in the universe. The beginning of this series of stories gives the origin of the Makaha Dog Society, which was a band of healers.

Wi heard about all this sickness so he sent his dog with a medicine bundle, a song and a dance.

Ksa, the spider spirit of wisdom and language, made many visits to earth. He became friends with Unktehila. This made Mapiyato very angry. He banished Ksa from the sky.

Iyan gave him a new name, Iktome.

Iktome became the trickster. He helped Unktehila create a birdlike dinosaur with bony jaws, lined with sharp-edged teeth. It was a feathered creature with long-clawed toes and sharp beak. It flew from place to place and then made its home in the jagged rocks of the Paha Sapa, the Black Hills.

Iktome and Unktehila formed a circle, which became an evil circle.

Before long the time came when the bearlike mammals were born. They could walk on two legs. They lived underneath the earth somewhere.

One day one of them reached light, through a cave. Mapiyato liked the mammal and invited it to attend a feast with the Star Council People. The mammal was so intelligent and helpful that Mapiyato gave it Iktome's place of wisdom.

Iyan thought for awhile and named it *hununpa*, meaning "having two legs."

In the regions under the world, Pte and Pta, the Bison People lived. Pte was called Wazi, the male bison. Pta was called Owankanka, the female bison.

They had neither winds, nor rains, nor the four seasons there in the nether regions where they lived.

To Wazi and Owankanka a very beautiful daughter was born. Iyan named her Ite.

It was not long after that Tate came to live among the Bison People. Tate admired Ite very much, and she in turn waited for his visits.

About that time, Ksapela appeared. He lusted after the young girl. He had plans to make her a slave to his mother and to his evil passion.

Ksapela was very humorous and told many funny stories to make people laugh. Ite clapped her hands the loudest.

Tate decided to visit his father. Upon hearing about the journey to Mapiyato, Ite gave Tate a lock of her long hair so that he wouldn't forget to come back.

While Tate was away, Ksapela persuaded the people to give a big feast for Wazi and Owankanka. The people were very impressed with Ksapela and returned his favors with another feast and another, until all their fields were empty of food.

They were near starvation and dying.

Ksapela led Ite into the empty fields and caused her to fall into a deep sleep. Ksapela told his brother Iya to watch over the girl while he went to eat. "When I return, I will make her my wife," he said.

Tate returned and found Ite crying because Iya was holding her prisoner. He called upon Wakinyan, who struck Iya with a flash of his eyes. Iya disappeared. Ksapela did not return when he saw what had happened to his brother.

Tate asked Ite to become his wife. When her parents had consented, Tate brought the rain.

Tate and Ite had four sons. The first born was the north wind. The second born was the west wind. The third born was the south wind. The fourth born was the east wind.

The Bison People had a big feast and gave each of the boys a name and a gift. Waziyata was the name given to the north wind. And he was given the color of white. He was to send snow and ice.

The color of black was given to the west wind. He was to control storms and floods. And he was given the name Wiyohpeyata.

The south wind was named Ito Kagata and was given the beautiful color of yellow. His responsibility was to melt the ice and snow.

The east wind was given the color of red and named Wiyohiyanpata. He was given the hardest responsibility. He was to guard the giant fireball.

They created the sixth sacred circle.

The seventh sacred circle is the separation of the seasons, which rotate in turn. This is where the heyoka *ceremony originated.*

One day Iktome sat in Ite's tipi and praised her beauty and smile. He told her that Wi had noticed her beauty.

But Ite only laughed at the trickster.

Iktome became angry and made a fine powder, a love potion made out of certain leaves, and put it in Ite's drinking water. Suddenly she became very vain and ignored her husband, Tate. She neglected her children and tipi.

Iktome went to visit Wi and his wife.

"*Kola*, how can I help you?" asked Wi.

"*Ho Kola*, you can help me by honoring this woman. She is a very good person," answered Iktome.

"Who may that be?" asked Hanhepi Wi.

"My friend is Ite, the wife of Tate. She is of the Bison-Pte people from beneath the world and is the mother of four important sons. The Star Council People consider this woman as ordinary and show her no respect. Respect must be shown this lovely woman."

"Let it be so. I will honor this woman at the next big feast," said Wi, "but you must bring her to me before the dance."

On the day of the great feast, Iktome helped Ite make herself more beautiful while her hungry children cried and cried. They had no fire to keep them warm.

Iktome took Ite to the great feast before any of the Star Council People had arrived. He placed Ite by Wi, who was at the head of the circle and who was the most important leader. Then Iktome rushed to Hanhepi Wi's tipi and told her that her husband wanted her to remove all her ornaments and best clothes and wear only her simplest clothes.

Iktome put out the fire and hid all the food in Hanhepi Wi's tipi. Then he reminded her that Wi still thought she was the most beautiful woman. The moon and sun's children were hungry and crying because they were cold. Their mother stopped listening to Iktome and built another fire. She cooked more food and warmed the tipi.

Iktome rushed to Wi and whispered to him that his wife, Hanhepi Wi, planned to embarrass him during the feast.

Ite had already used her charm and won Wi. He smiled at her, and he noticed her beauty. He was so dazzled by her beauty that he had forgotten all about his wife.

Hanhepi Wi arrived late for the feast. When she saw her husband with Ite, she covered her face in sorrow and shame, turned away and cried and cried.

Tate, learning that he had lost his wife to Wi, blackened the four faces of his children and his own face as a sign of mourning.

Suddenly, Wi realized what was happening and went home to his wife, Hanhepi Wi. But she would not uncover her face.

All the Star Council People still at the feast were laughing. Iktome laughed the loudest and the longest.

Mapiyato became very angry and decided to punish all four of Iktome's friends and to leave him until the very last. Ite's punishment was the most severe since she had neglected her tipi, forgotten her children, tormented Tate.

She was always to travel alone and never have any friends or relatives. Her face on the right side stayed pretty, but the other side became very ugly. It was so ugly that it terrified everyone.

Mapiyato told her that her next child would be born before its time and that he was going to be very mischievous, like Iktome. Yumnimni was to be his name, meaning "whirlwind," the symbol for lovemaking.

Wi was ordered to govern the day forever and was told he would never see his wife's face again, even when she came near him every month.

Hanhepi Wi would hide her face forever and was to

remain no longer with Wi. She lost most of her luminous light because she mourned and grew very thin, so thin that she became a tiny crescent. Gradually, she became herself again, but each time she passed Wi, she cried and grew thin and weary again.

Tate was asked to take his four sons and leave and travel to the four corners of the world and not to look for his wife, Anong Ite, "the two-faced one."

Iktome was banished from the Star Council People and sent to live alone in a cold country where Wi did not provide him with heat nor make things grow. Iktome was always hungry and cold.

Tate gave a feast and invited all the Star Council People.

"The sons of Tate are sacred," said Mapiyato, "and they shall be messengers in all ceremonies."

Then he gave his grandsons new names.

Waziyata was now Yata, the first son. Wiyohpeyata was named Eya, the second son. Ito Kagata was called Okaga, the third son. Wiyohiyanpata was Yanpa, the fourth son.

Tate's smallest son was called Yumni.

The four oldest sons of Tate set out to circle the four directions in the universe.

On the first night Okaga found the sweet grass growing along the water. He brought it back to camp.

The following night, they encountered the swallow, and asked that bird to lead them to Wakinyan's home.

"I am his messenger," the swallow told them. "Whoever looks at him becomes *heyoka* and forever after will act the opposite. Do you still wish to see him?"

"I wish to look at him," Eya said.

The swallow led Eya to Wakinyan's tipi. Immediately, there rose from the tipi a shapeless thing like smoke. It was without a head, but had a huge eye. Its teeth were like a cutting stone. It had great wings but no body. Instead of legs or feet, it had talons.

Eya stared at it in amazement and laughed. Then he stood on his head and walked on his hands. Eya was now *heyoka*, the thunder dreamer.

"Go now with your brothers," said Wakinyan.

Eya, the second son, had taken the first son's birthright and selected the first direction, which was the west where the sun goes. He took the swallow as his messenger.

Yata, the first son, became angry and turned to ice and could not move, so his direction was the north. A magpie became his messenger.

Yanpa, the fourth son, found his direction in the east. The meadowlark became his messenger and brought the Olakota language. The meadowlark sings in the spring, "*Ungle pelo, ungle pelo.*"

Okaga, the third son, set his direction in the south. The owl was his messenger. His path is the path of the dead. Souls smell like sweet grass.

The seventh sacred circle is now complete.

These stories contain the origin of the Makaha Brotherhood of the Flute, men whose playing of love songs women could not resist. The stories also establish the path of the dead.

When it was nighttime, Yanpa, the east wind, sat on the edge of the world and made music with his flute. The music was so beautiful that the stars came near him, paused and listened to him. Many of them clustered about him.

One bright star lingered near and cried a warning to

the others, "Don't stay, lest you be overcome by the music of his love songs."

The others did not heed her and each longed to have Yanpa for her own husband.

Mapiyato saw that the stars would not heed the warning. He gave Yanpa's music the power to melt them so that they became like a huge cloud.

"You shall be stars no more," said Mapiyato. "You shall forever remain like a cloud, wandering around the edge of the world in search of Yanpa and his Indian love songs."

These stars became the pathway to the tipi of Unci, the great grandmother, where *wacanga*, the sweet grass, grows.

The Milky Way, a huge pinwheel of hot, young stars, became a path to the realm beyond. Unci guards the entrance of death. She has a tattoo on her forehead, a symbol of the four directions.

She is a weaver who keeps adding to the medicine basket. By day, she weaves the water which flows from the Milky Way by way of the Little Dipper into the Big Dipper, forming clouds on the medicine basket.

Sometimes Unci weaves the raindrops and the snowflakes together and adds arrowheads, spear points, thumbstones and scrapers as decorations in her design. By night, her dog unravels all her precious work, causing severe rain and snowstorms. Thus, the arrowheads, spear points, thumbstones and scrapers drop to the earth's valleys and rivers.

Earth, Gravity

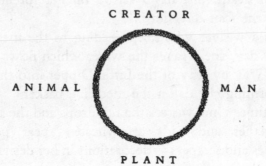

CREATOR

ANIMAL   MAN

PLANT

The Great Circle

4 / CYCLES OF SEVEN:

Life finds its rhythm

The creation stories from the first world are rich in symbols, foremost among which is the circle. To my people, the circle is the basic symbol of the universe. The tipi is a circle. The drum is a circle. All our dances are circles. We believe in eternal recurrence, which is what the circle tells us. As Grandfather Black Elk has said, everything in the universe tries to be round.

At the center of the circle is the creator, whom we call Wakan Tanka, or sometimes the grandfather, Tunkashila, or the Great Spirit or Great Mystery. The center of the circle is the masculine principle, the potential within all things. Getting to the center of the circle is the feminine principle, the soul in motion, love. This is the concept that guides our lives. Every life is a circle. And within every life are smaller circles. A part of our lives goes full circle every seven years. We speak of living in cycles of seven.

At the beginning of a cycle, we are happy, productive and creative. Toward the end of the seven years, our energy starts to wane. Many times we find ourselves sick. We may injure ourselves or be mentally unstable. To get through the end of a cycle, we attend many sweat lodge ceremonies to gain physical and spiritual strength. We become aware of our limitations and how to cope with them. The elders are always available to give us advice or take us into their homes.

A Makaha child, embarking on her first cycle of seven, is joyously received after much thought and preparation have gone into her arrival. Often her mother, when she is first pregnant, will choose a great personage as the model for the child. She thinks of this wise and esteemed figure every day and imparts all his or her goodness to the child growing in her womb. She keeps to herself so that she can control the impulses the child receives. She walks in grand and beautiful settings. She prays and celebrates new life.

If the mother carries the baby high or if she sees a falling star, the child will be a boy.

Certain kinds of animals can confer gifts on the unborn, and others can affect the child adversely. A rabbit, for instance, can cause harelip in a child. We say that the rabbit charmed the mother and gave the baby its own features.

Grandmothers and other female relatives sew clothing for the baby. The father's sister makes the cradle board, usually of cedar. Many women weave the cradle reeds.

At the birth, all the people remain silent and keep their mouths shut, respectful of the baby's *niya*. All the lights are low. When the contractions are coming quickly, the woman squats and braces herself against a pole. A woman chosen to escort the child into the world holds the baby's head so that the entrance into the world is gentle and not too fast. She clears the baby's respiratory passages and lays him or her on the mother's stomach. Then she gently massages the newborn. She cleanses the baby's body with warm pure oil processed from puppy fat.

When the baby's navel cord falls off, it goes into the turtle-shaped pouch, along with sweet grass, kinnikinnick, sage and cedar. A boy's pouch is pinned to the shoulder of his shirt. A girl's pouch is pinned to the inside of her dress.

The newborn immediately hears lullabies telling of magnificent exploits in hunting and war. Everyone tells the child about the model his or her mother had chosen and about the greatness of that person. A boy is told that he is the future defender of his people, whose lives may depend on his courage and skill. A girl is called the future mother of the noble race.

The baby receives a name at the naming ceremony. During this ritual, a girl wears a tiny white stone around her neck. A boy wears a black stone. The stones symbolize Iyan, who names all things.

I was only a month old when I got my Indian name. It was from a grandfather who was Cheyenne. He told my grandmother to call me Wapaha, which means war bonnet. He had a vision about the name for me.

Childhood is a holy time. My people regard the child as deserving special treatment because of having come over from the other side, or the spirit world, so recently.

Traditionally, the child's mother worried only about the development of her baby. The father provided food, shelter and other basic necessities. Families were limited to two or three children, born five years apart. A woman practiced birth control by drinking the juice of a sacred plant, one that appeared to her in a vision.

The grandparents were responsible for the child's education to the age of four. They actually took the children and cared for them. When the parents took over after the first four years, they reinforced all that the grandparents had taught. They encouraged the child to serve the people, to respect the elders, to share, to be honest, to have pride, to achieve, to honor peace and wisdom and to walk a spiritual path.

Teaching outside the family came from tribal elders, who were experts in survival. They focused on the future of the tribe and told the young how to perpetuate the ways of the people. They told all the old stories and retold them so the tradition would live in generations to come.

At age seven the child begins the second cycle of life. This is the cycle during which boys and girls begin to see their different roles. Traditionally, a girl was taught by her mother and grandmother to prepare food and care for the household. She sewed her first tipi, moccasins and leggings. Toward the end of this cycle, she began her visits to the moon hut.

The moon hut was big enough for one person, and the girl dug a hole about twelve inches down to sit on for the duration of her menstrual period. She was not permitted to touch food or anything else. Someone came in and fed her. Any cloths soaked in menstrual blood, she would bundle up and hang in a tree. The bundle eventually dried up and blew away.

When her period was over, she used sage to clean herself off, covered the hole, took the little hut down and went to the sweat lodge ceremony.

The isolation of the moon hut provided a time of great relaxation. It was necessary for the woman to be away from everyone else during this time because menstrual blood is a sacred substance, carrying unused lives. That substance has great power and must be tended to carefully. With the careless way women today treat their menstrual materials, it is no wonder that there is so much trouble in the world. I advise women to isolate themselves as much as possible during this time.

One Makaha ceremony demonstrates the power of the menses. This is called *kumugha*. The medicine man uses this ritual on "someone who has no ears," someone who pays no attention or is disrespectful. The medicine man asks for a hair from the head of a menstruating woman. He puts this hair on his palm, and he blows on it. The hair goes directly to its target's knees, no matter how far away that person is. He immediately feels it. His knees buckle. He has to participate in a sweat lodge before he can walk again.

Indian boys during their second cycle of seven had to run long distances to develop their speed and endurance. They learned to use the bow and arrow and to track game. They hunted for birds, turtles and rabbits. They learned to kill only when their families needed food. They took care of the horses.

It is around age nine that Indian children begin to participate in two of the great rituals, vision seeking and the sweat lodge.

Adulthood comes with the beginning of the third cycle. By age fifteen, an Indian should understand his or her purpose in life and know the beliefs and ways of the people.

Arranged marriages were the custom. The two families would exchange gifts to mark the occasion.

The husband would comb and braid his wife's hair every day. He would then mark her part with red powder called *wase*, or ocher.

Indian women were very wise. They knew that a marriage could not sustain high romance. They did not expect immediate sexual fulfillment and were prepared to spend years adjusting sexually to their husbands.

It was traditional that the oldest girl in a family

became the first wife, and her sisters were married in the order of their ages. All women married.

Both the husband and the wife remained strongly attached to their parents.

It is during the third cycle that people participate in the sun dance ritual.

The fourth cycle, beginning at age twenty-one, is a time for developing ties outside the immediate family and for organizing ceremonies. This is the age during which the Makaha concentrates on his status in the community.

The ritual for the making of relatives is important to this cycle. Everything that a person can do to extend his family adds to his influence and the importance of his ceremonies.

The fifth cycle, from ages twenty-eight to thirty-four, is a time of difficulty. Change is the rule here. Long ago, it was said that the deer men bothered a woman in her fifth cycle. A deer man has a magnetic personality. He is extremely handsome and seductive. Once he has led a woman away from her family, he leaps up and runs, like a deer.

One evening I was outside hanging clothes when I saw a deer standing behind some trees in the back yard. I lived in a crowded neighborhood. A deer was an unusual sight. I went back to hanging my clothes. When I looked up again, I saw a man in the deer's place. I panicked and ran. My dog was spooked, too.

The deer man appeared to me several times after that. For six months every time I went to a pow wow, I would see him in the crowd. I got such an urge to follow him the first time that I told my husband what I was feeling. He took me away immediately. The next time I saw the man at a pow wow, he got up from the drums he was playing and started to move away from the crowd. His magnetism was so strong that I had to hold on to my aunt's arm while one of my boys ran to get my husband. I was obsessed with the man until a medicine man came to pray with me for several days. That broke the deer man's spell.

Men in the fifth cycle have similar problems with deer women. My husband went outside one winternight because he heard a woman calling to him. When he looked at her, he was hypnotized and started wandering after her. She began to lose her power because the temperature was twenty-seven degrees below zero. When my husband started to realize how cold he was, she turned into a deer and jumped across a ditch and over a fence into the woods.

Men, however, tend to have most of their experiences with deer women during their sixth cycle, ages thirty-five to forty-one. By then their wives, having already battled the deer men, can better understand what they are going through.

Women have to realize during this time that their role is to help men regain their wisdom. One way we can help them is to have purifying ceremonies for them. Recently, a male friend of mine in his sixth cycle began appearing to me. I was embarrassed because I considered him a brother. He sent a bundle of hair. My mother and I burned it with sweet grass, sage and cedar. He sent another bundle. Two of my sons burned it, according to my instructions. I keep finding tobacco ties, offerings from him, in my pockets, on my bed, on the floor. All I can do is continue to have ceremonies for him. He is restless.

The seventh cycle, ages forty-two to forty-eight, is basically a cooling-off period. People are calmer and wiser. They become grandparents. They hold positions of trust and importance in the community. They take renewed interest in life. Turmoil is behind them.

The rest of their lives they will experience the cycles of seven over the course of whatever time is allotted to them. These remaining cycles will be characterized by the waxing and waning of energy, but will bring no major changes until death.

Puberty Rituals

5 / THE FIRST WORLD
INTERPRETED:

Two great rituals bind creation to creator

My ancestors practiced the seven great rituals, as I have said. Two of them are drawn from the creation stories of the first world. These are the throwing of the ball, *tapa wanka yap*, and the preparing of a girl for womanhood, *ishna ta awi cha lowan*.

These rituals, with their origins in the oldest of the creation stories, are also the two that are least practiced today. In fact, I know of no one at all who practices the throwing of the ball.

My grandmother has a beaded ball that was used in the throwing of the ball ritual. It belonged to her father, the last of our family who participated in that ceremony. The ball is made of buffalo hair, covered with buffalo hide and brightly beaded.

The ball represents the universe before it broke apart, the center of all things, the source of all knowledge.

The ancient ritual was in the form of a game. The materials necessary for the game were a pipe, some tobacco, sweet grass, a spotted eagle feather, a knife, a hatchet, some sage, a buffalo skull and the ball.

My information about this ritual comes from Black Elk in *The Sacred Pipe* and from what my grandmother remembers.

The rite took place in a consecrated tipi with sage scattered all over the floor. The leader sat at the west, facing east. He burned sweet grass over a live coal and offered a prayer of gratitude to the creator, Wakan Tanka. Then he passed each piece of equipment through the sweet grass smoke for purification.

As the sun came up, he marked out the place for his ceremonial platform by burying a hatchet at each of the four points of a square in front of him. Next he took a knife and scraped a pile of earth from each place he had struck with the hatchet. He took the loose earth and scattered it over the site and spread it evenly with the spotted eagle feather. Then he drew a cross, from west to east and from north to south. Next he laid two lines of tobacco along the lines of the cross, and he painted the tobacco red. His completed platform represented the universe and all that is in it.

He sang a sacred song while a drummer drummed.

Meanwhile, a young girl had been brought into the tipi by her father and, after moving clockwise around it, went to sit by the leader. Her role was to stand and hold the ball in her left hand while raising her right hand to the heavens. She was chosen for her purity and innocence.

The ball was red and blue with a dot at each of the four quarters. As the girl held the ball, the leader prayed, thanking the creator for a loving presence in the universe and for spiritual enlightenment.

Then the girl left the tipi to begin tossing the ball. The leader followed her out. He carried a buffalo skull painted with two red lines, one around it and one from between the horns to between the eyes. The buffalo skull represented the Bison People, who gave the ritual to the "two-leggeds."

All the people were gathered in a circle outside. The girl threw the ball first to the west. Whoever caught it was considered blessed. The girl then threw the ball to the north, the east and the south. The three who caught the ball at those points were also greatly blessed. The last toss was straight up, and there was a great scramble for the ball. When it was returned to the girl, the game was over.

The leader offered a prayer of dedication.

In *The Sacred Pipe*, Black Elk said that the ball descending was the power of the creator coming down to the people. He lamented the fact that in his day (he lived from 1863 to 1950) very few people tried to catch the ball. He was saddened by such spiritual indifference because, as he said, "It is the two-legged men alone who, if they purify and humiliate themselves, may become one with—or may know—Wakan Tanka." He predicted that the end of a great cycle was rapidly approaching. He thought he was living in the last days of the fourth world.

Some people consider the throwing of the ball a puberty ritual since a virgin has such a central part in it. The main puberty ritual, however, is that of preparing a girl for womanhood.

A Makaha girl's coming of age is a significant event, and her parents begin preparing her for it when she is eight or nine. That's when they ask an old woman to start watching the child. That same woman will continue with the girl until she is married. In the old days people married at the age of twelve or thirteen, so the old woman's job was very short.

My grandmother hired a certain woman elder in the tribe to protect me. Until I was eighteen, she was always with me.

The old woman represents the bear, because she keeps the girl's virginity. With our people, it's the bear who is the protector of virgins.

When the girl is still young, her parents have to choose the tribal elder who will perform the coming into womanhood ceremony. They take the man an offering of tobacco and ask him to think about how he will perform the ceremony for their daughter.

Then they start preparing the gifts they will give this man once he performs the ceremony. They have to give him a whole buckskin outfit, plus many blankets and household goods. In the old days, he got horses.

This old man will spend many years going to sweat lodges or even vision seeking to see what kind of ceremony he will perform for this child. He will be an adviser to her parents.

A vision may tell him that the girl should wear certain colors or eat certain foods. He may even suggest a name change for her if his vision tells him to.

My granddaughter, Valyssa Yellow Wolf Adams, is only a year old, and already I'm looking around to see what elderly man would be worthy of doing this ceremony for her. I've also prepared the white eagle feather that my granddaughter will receive when she enters womanhood. An elderly man gave it to me and said it was for her.

All of these things lead up to the girl's first menstruation and are called *hunkapi*, preparation for the menstual cycle.

As I mentioned in the last chapter, the moon hut ritual, based on the story about the banishment of Hanpetu, the symbol of fertility, was a monthly occurrence for menstruating women. This ritual died out with my grandmother's generation.

After the girl's first menstruation, there is a celebration marking the end of *hunkapi*. First, the girl is taken to a sweat lodge for a purification ceremony. Then the old woman sings the *mato awicalowanpi* song. This is the song to *hununpa*, the bear, protector of virgins. The song is a petition to the bear to continue watching over the girl.

After she hears this song, a girl must be careful where she urinates. From then on, the scent of her urine will bring all the male animals around. Women who are not careful of where they urinate are considered promiscuous.

At this ceremony, which is informal and for family only, both the old woman and the old man chosen to guide the girl through this time give her advice. Afterwards, her family puts on a feast and gives gifts to the two advisers.

The next ceremony for the girl is *ishna*, presentation of the white plume from the breast of the spotted eagle.

The parents decide when to have this ceremony. This is for the whole community and involves the giving of gifts to many people.

Ishna is a preparation for marriage and children. All the people in the community gather.

The old woman takes the girl to the ceremony. She leads her inside a tipi where new clothes have been laid out for her. The old woman makes a fire of sage and sweet grass and runs the clothes through the smoke to purify them. Then she helps the girl change into these clothes.

The old woman paints the girl's face red, symbolizing rebirth and the earth. Women represent the earth, which makes everything grow.

Four men bring a bear robe, and they carry the girl on it to the center of the ceremonial grounds. The men put the robe and the girl down, and she sits on the robe in the center of the people while various members of the community talk about her ancestors.

Many elder people will stand up and talk for the girl. They will tell her whole family history. Everyone is seated in a circle. Anyone who stands up and says something good about the girl will receive a gift from her family. Everyone wants to say something good. They can say as much as they want. Nobody ever stops them from talking. Sometimes this ceremony seems to go on forever.

Since the ceremony takes place out in the open, it's usually done during the summer, during August.

After the many and various accounts of the girl's family history, the elder chosen to conduct the ceremony talks about all the accomplishments of the girl. He tells Wakan Tanka that she has done all that was required of her.

He takes sage and sweet grass and burns them and holds the smoke over the girl. He brings stalks of corn, which represent the making of relatives, a ritual that the girl will perform later in her life. The corn gives her the power to do so when she is ready.

One of the people who has spoken on behalf of the girl gives her the white plume from the breast of the spotted eagle. He pins it to her hair. He has prepared for this moment by going to a sweat lodge and praying for the girl.

The eagle plume is attached to a circle made out of porcupine quills. It is confirmation that the girl has committed herself to the service of the people. It symbolizes her intention to practice the virtues of kindness, generosity and truthfulness.

The eagle plume is the only feather a virgin is allowed to wear. When a woman loses her virginity, she puts the eagle plume aside for another woman in her family.

Once the eagle plume has been pinned to her hair, the girl hears her honor song, usually for the first time. An honor song is unique to each individual. It is sung any time that person deserves recognition. It is sung for the last time on the day the person is buried.

My honor song was put together for my *ishna* ceremony. It says that I am a caretaker for my people and that I come from a long line of powerful people.

Next, the ceremonial pipe of the girl's family goes around. It is presented to the four winds or directions. Everybody smokes it. The girl is the last to smoke it.

Then the drummers come in, the honor song is sung again, and the dance starts. The girl leads the dance, which is done clockwise in a circle. Her parents or grandparents are on either side of her, then behind them are all the girl's other relatives, then all her friends.

After the dance, everyone goes into a sweat lodge. A buffalo skull is at the entrance to the sweat lodge. It represents the Bison People and also the White Buffalo Calf Woman, who comes in the fourth world.

When the sweat lodge ceremony is finished, the girl's family invites everyone to a feast and a giveaway. Presents go to all the people who have done things for the girl during the time that led up to this occasion, to all those who spoke on her behalf, to all the elders, all the widows, all the orphans and all other friends.

Makaha boys also have a coming of age ritual during which they receive the feather from the breast of the spotted eagle.

Long ago, a boy had to catch his own eagle. He would scout for eagle nests, and one day he would bring home an eaglet. He would feed and care for that eaglet until the grandfathers decided it was time for his ceremony.

Then the boy would put the sacred braided rope around the eagle's neck and slowly choke it. The boy would remove all the feathers. He would put the eagle's head atop a staff, which is the memorial to the life of that eagle and which the boy would keep until the day of his death. He would make the wing bones into flutes for his sun dance ceremonies. He would save the eagle claws, which are tied to a strip of buckskin and used during ceremonies and in talking circles. The wings from the eagle would become his fans, to spread the smoke of sage and sweet grass. The tail feathers would become the bustle of his dance costume. If he had a vision, he could make a war bonnet from twenty-eight of the eagle's feathers. Only those who have a vision that they are to be leaders of the people make such a headdress.

When my grandson, Justin Yellow Wolf Adams, goes through this ritual, he will use eagle feathers, claws, wings and flutes that have been in my family for generations. He will be guided by an elderly man in his preparations and public ritual. He will also have the protection of the bear, as all virgin boys do.

 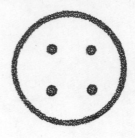

Sweet Grass: cleansing,
prayer, healing

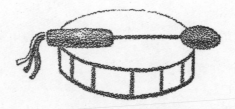

Life Pulse, Drum:
heartbeat of the earth;
buffalo hide stretched
over hollowed logs;
used in every ceremony

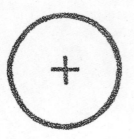

Grandmother
(*Unoi*, tatoo on forehead)

6 / MAKAHA SYMBOLISM:

A culture finds the key to its traditions

Symbolism is the storehouse of cultural memory. The secrets of my ancestors have been locked in symbols. My generation has lost the key to those symbols that keep our traditions alive.

The bright beadwork designs and the props used in ceremonies are all poetic expressions of the relationship between the people and the universe. We repeat the designs and use the props without knowing what they mean. I want to begin restoring the power of our symbols.

The Sioux medicine man Lame Deer, in *Seeker of Visions*, published in 1974, wrote that for the Sioux, symbols are part of nature. "We try to understand them, not with the head but with the heart, and we need no more than a hint to give us meaning. What to you seems commonplace, to us appears wondrous through symbolism. This is funny, because we don't even have a word for symbolism, yet we are all wrapped up in it. You have the word, but that is all."

For my ancestors, signs received from nature provided the key to understanding the universe and promoted a reverent acceptance of their rightful place in it.

Many of these signs are evident in the creation stories of the first world.

The drum, for instance, which we use in all our ceremonies and which is often the only instrument in a ceremony, comes from Iyan's giving his daughter Maka a heart. The beat of that heart is the beat of the drum. The drum beat is the life force, the earth's heart, the rhythm of gravity. The drum's shape reflects the circle of life.

It is made from hollowed out logs and struck with a wooden stick, linking it to trees, which my ancestors called the "standing people." It is covered with stretched buffalo hide, a tie to the animal world, or the world of the "four-leggeds." All of the world, therefore, is in that drum. And whoever plays the drum becomes the channel between earth and heaven.

The drum beat is the pulse of the keeping of the soul, making of relatives, sweat lodge and sun dance rituals. The Makaha used it also in the ghost dance and the naming ceremony.

Every Makaha woman had a divorce drum outside the tipi. All she had to do was strike the drum three times, and her husband had to pick up his personal belongings and leave.

Sweet grass, which Okaga, the south wind, introduced, is a part of almost all our rituals. Its life began when the world settled into the four seasons. It grows in the plains and mountains and can reach five feet in height. We cut it, braid it and dry it and then burn it to chase away evil spirits.

The burning of sweet grass is a prayer, sent to

heaven on the smoke. Wakan Tanka is nature and understands fire and smoke much better than words. When I burn sweet grass, I don't mouth words. I just sit there and watch the smoke.

Sweet grass has universal use among American Indian tribes. It is for prayer and for cleansing. It can be a healing agent.

There are several other stories about the origin of sweet grass. One is that the Little People, who begin to appear regularly in stories from the second world, became so fascinated by their reflection in a pool that they pined away, leaving only a grass bearing their sweet fragrance, a memory of their vanity.

Another story is that sweet grass sprang up wherever the White Buffalo Calf Woman's tears fell as she changed from a red buffalo to yellow, to black, to white. White Buffalo Calf Woman is a major figure among the Sioux and appears in stories from the fourth world.

Sage, like sweet grass, is a symbol of cleanliness and purity. Tate, motion, son of the sky, gets his power from the sage plant.

Sage is a necessary part of every sacred ceremony. It is particularly important in the sun dance because the dancers chew it to alleviate their thirst. They wear crowns of sage. The silver-leaf sage plant is the incense of the seven sacred rituals. The leaf never dries out; it stays moist forever.

Another story about the origin of sage as a symbol involves the Little People again. The custom among them was to offer gifts each year to the White Buffalo Calf Woman. A poor girl, when her turn to give came, had nothing to offer. She plucked some weeds growing along her path and laid them at the White Buffalo Calf Woman's altar. So pure and fervent was her faith that the dry brown weeds turned to beautiful silver.

The four colors, together with the four directions, play a major role in Makaha culture. These are the sons of Tate.

Black is the color of the west. It represents the end, the final vow. When we do things in the dark, they are final things.

Hanhepi Wi, when she would not show her face because of her shame over Wi's behavior, gave us black as the symbol of mourning. So did Tate when he painted his sons' faces after their mother's infidelity.

The west is where the thunder being dwells and where the rain starts. People who have an affinity for the west are *heyoka*, those who do everything backwards. According to Lame Deer, "Everything in nature moves in a certain way that whites call clockwise. Only the thunder beings move in a contrary manner—counterclockwise." They are the sacred clowns. They wear bald eagle feathers, for this is the kind of eagle associated with the west. People who have had visions of the bald eagle must follow the *heyoka* ritual or lightning strikes them and thunder stuffs them with grass. The *heyoka* can control storms, either summoning them or diverting them from a destructive path.

White is the color of the north. It is a cleansing, purifying, strengthening power. As winter cleanses the earth of the weak, white and the north teach a person endurance and courage. White is the color of wisdom, which comes from encounters with the hard things of life. The north sends tests.

The white eagle is the sign of the north. A white eagle feather appears in a vision to people who later become healers. These days, the white eagle has replaced the bear as the symbol of wisdom.

Red is the color of the east, the place where new life rises up with each day. Peace and light come from the east. Blood and birth are from the east. The spotted eagle brings all these things. Spotted eagle feathers are used in all ceremonies. Spotted eagle feathers bring insight and visions.

Yellow is the color of the south. The sun is strongest when one faces south. The golden eagle stands for the peak of life, warmth, understanding and ability. The golden eagle escorts the soul on its death trail to the Milky Way.

The eagle is the most visible creature in Makaha culture. In the first world, after he created Maka, the earth, Iyan gave her a gift, which was the sense of sight. The gift came in the form of an eagle feather. The eagle is a symbol of vision, both material and spiritual. The eagle's claws are a symbol of strength.

In stories from the third world, the people come from an eagle. After a great flood, only a girl is left. She is carried away by an eagle, and they mate, producing all who walk the earth now.

All animals are very important to the Makaha. The bison was essential to the existence of my ancestors. It provided food, clothing and shelter. It is thus accorded a place of honor in the Makaha pantheon. It is called a people, i.e., the Bison People. The Bison People provide everything to the "two-leggeds."

The male bison Wazi is the keeper of ceremonies. His wife Owankanka liked to spread gossip, and his daughter Anong Ite was two-faced. We don't use the female bison in our rituals. When the White Buffalo Calf Woman comes, in the fourth world, the female is restored to power and dignity.

The buffalo is central to many rituals and is the subject of innumerable legends. If I have a vision of a buffalo associated with a certain person, I know that person will have a role somehow in preserving Makaha ceremonies.

I have a psychologist friend who did not believe in any of my visions. She thought they were some kind of abnormality. Then one night when she turned out her lamp, she saw a little turquoise buffalo glowing on her wall. The next day she asked a friend what that buffalo might have meant. He asked her which tribe had the buffalo as its symbol. She remembered what I had said about the buffalo, and she called me. I was in the hospital, recovering from emergency surgery performed the night before. Now every time something is wrong in my family, my psychologist friend sees that little turquoise buffalo.

The buffalo represents the four ages. My people believe that at the beginning of the world, the buffalo was placed in the west to hold back the waters. Each year this buffalo loses one strand of hair, and each age he loses one leg. When all his hair and all his legs are gone, the waters will rush in and flood the world. Then the cycle will begin again.

The spider was originally the spirit of knowledge, and his thread was the path for all life. However, the spider got too clever for the gods and was banished, becoming the trickster, Iktome. All children's stories that have to do with the teaching of values are Iktome stories. In the stories of the second world, the water spider brings fire. The spider in the fourth world reveals the basic geometric patterns that the Oglala use in their beadwork.

The man to whom I go for advice all the time has the power of the spider. His name is Bill Good Voice Elk. He is a very strong medicine man. He was nine years old when he went out vision seeking. The spider came to him then. Spiders will come to him all the time. They are his helpers.

When the spider was banished from the Star Council, the bear took over as the spirit of wisdom. *Hununpa* protects purity, keeps it from becoming cleverness. In the stories of the second world, the bear taught the use of the bow and arrow.

My grandmother's great-grandmother had the power of the bear. She was a healer. Her name was Mary Standing Soldier.

She was just a little girl out picking berries when a bear chased her. She realized she couldn't outrun him, so she got behind a big tree. Every time the bear reached around to take a swipe at her, she would strike at his paws with her little hatchet. Finally, she had cut both paws off, and the bear bled to death.

Her family took the bear robe and the claws. This is how she received her bear powers.

She was of the Cheyenne people, and she lived during the days when the white man was in his fierce struggle with the native peoples of the Plains. Mary Standing Soldier was only about four and a half feet tall, a tiny woman. When any of her people were struck by either arrows or bullets, she would go to them and make noises like a bear, *mato wapiya*. She used the powers of the bear to remove the arrow or bullet from the wounded person's body and to get him back on his feet.

My grandmother, who was seven when Mary Standing Soldier died, remembers that she had long hair all over her body, just like a bear.

In addition to her bear claws, Mary Standing Soldier carried the hand of her youngest brother. He was killed during the battle of Little Big Horn. She had a little box made of buckskin. She had a bundle in that box. My grandmother was always very curious about what was in that bundle.

One day when Mary Standing Soldier was away, my young grandmother opened the box and unwrapped the bundle. She remembers the hand as being very dry.

When Mary Standing Soldier returned, she told my grandmother that she knew about her getting into the little box. Then she told the story of whose hand it was. When she died, she was buried with her little box. Carrying the hand may have been the Cheyenne form of the keeping of the soul ritual.

Our family still has the bear claws that Mary Standing Soldier carried. My youngest son Melvin used them in his sun dance.

The owl is the symbol of death. *Nagi*, the vigilant and wandering part of the soul, can take the form of the owl to forewarn of injury or death. The only person I ever heard of who had the power of the owl was Crazy Horse. The owl gave him the power to kill.

The dog is the symbol of healing. It was the first animal to bring healing powers to the people. Even today, we use the dog in all our healing ceremonies.

When my grandmother went to Bill Good Voice Elk for a cure of her arthritis, he told her to take a dog's paw and put it by a creek. We wrapped it and put it in a tree. This was an offering after the *yuwipi*, or healing ceremony.

People call us the dog eaters, in a derogatory manner. We do eat puppies after many of our ceremonies. This gives us strength from the dog. It's the same concept as communion in the Catholic Church. Since the dog was the first to offer itself as a healer of humankind, it has much spiritual power.

My aunt has a puppy farm. She has several female dogs. She selects puppies and feeds them separately, giving them food that people eat. These are the puppies that are sacrificed. The meat is white and tastes like pork.

We make offerings to the spirit of the dog and are very reverent in the way we take its life.

Unci is Iyan's wife. We call her the grandmother. She is the guardian of the entrance to the other side. She waits for the golden eagle with its soul bundle. She takes care of the village on the other side. She makes sure you have a tipi waiting when you arrive there and that your food is ready. She helps you make the transition to your new life on the other side.

Unci lives in the Milky Way, the path the souls take on their way back to the seven stars of the Big Dipper. Unci waits at the end of the path and admits those who have a certain tattoo on their foreheads or on their arms.

My grandmother has this tattoo on her forehead. It is a small cross, the symbol of the four directions.

She had the tattoo made in the old way. A spot on her forehead was rubbed raw. The design was pricked into her skin with bone needles from the penis of a beaver. Then false indigo was rubbed in.

Her father won the privilege of tattooing her because of his lavish giveaways on her behalf. Everyone who has this kind of tattoo is a member of the Society of Those Blessed by the Night.

Unci sees that tattoo and lets the golden eagle pass with his soul bundle.

The flute is used during the sun dance and during courting rituals. It is the instrument of love. It can be made from the wing bone of an eagle or from a cedar branch.

Mountains

War Shield:
from the Little People

Snake (*Ksa*)

Animal, Buffalo

7 / CREATION STORIES FROM THE SECOND WORLD:

The people receive their names

In the creation stories from the second world, the bear loses his place among the Star Council People because he breaks a sacred trust. He is banished to earth, taking the people from the Big Dipper with him. Each star in the Big Dipper is connected to a tribe. This is one of the origins of our sacred number seven: The seven stars in the Big Dipper create the seven Olakota-speaking tribes.

The second world stories are about the coming of people onto earth and the different names the people took as they evolved. The stories touch also on the origin of places known to the Makaha.

Until the people from the Big Dipper mixed fully with the people on earth, the earth people were wandering about without souls. Our souls come from the stars.

One nation lived on the seven stars called the Big Dipper. Another nation lived on the North Star.

The North Star leader was a giant whose name was Wazia Wichaghpi Owanjihan. One day he challenged one of the leaders from the Big Dipper, struck him across the heart and then ran. The leaders from the other six stars chased him.

The giant injured the one closing in on him. The injured one ran bravely on, even though blood covered his chest and face. He ran so well, in fact, that the other five stayed in the chase only by following his bloody trail.

Soon the giant stopped and challenged the one he had injured. As they struggled, the other five got close enough to see the giant kill their brother.

The giant ran again. This time the bloody trail came from a cut in his heel.

The giant managed to kill all the rest of his pursuers, one by one. Each time he killed, he received a new wound. He was getting slower and slower until, after he killed the last one, he laid down to sleep. When he awoke, he saw that twilight had come. He got up and continued to travel. Along the path he met the bear.

"Where are you going with such a sad face?" the bear asked.

"I am going to see who those new stars are," the giant said.

"Ho," responded the bear. "I think I can help you. Those new stars that you see are the leaders that chased you yesterday."

"How can I catch up with them?" the giant asked.

"They are far ahead of you. They have fled with all their people. But soon they will all get tired and want to rest."

The giant told the bear that he was hungry and wanted something to eat right away. The bear fed him.

Then the bear told him how he could get rid of the other leaders for good. He gave the giant twelve arrows from Wakinyan's lightning. And he warned him: "If you fail to get rid of those leaders, you will fall out of the dome of Mapiyato."

That night the giant started out and came to the place where the other leaders were hurrying back and forth. He bent his bow and took careful aim. He sent five of the arrows toward his enemies. In spite of his skill as an archer, he did not hit anyone.

The other leaders shot back at him, but they missed their target, too.

The giant then bent his bow another seven times and sent the arrows of Wakinyan flying. Suddenly, the seven leaders of the Big Dipper burst into flame and went spiraling toward the earth.

The giant was excited over his victory until he heard a voice from the sky telling him: "You will remain alone on the North Star forever. Your job will be to guide all travelers. Since you have misused the arrows, the reflections of the Big Dipper people will follow you forever."

The giant was sad. He grew sadder as he watched the bear falling toward earth.

When the bear reached earth, he heard the voice of Mapiyato telling him: "You are banished from the sky forever and will remain on earth. Your name will be *mato*. Your job will be to look after all these people who have fled their homes in the stars."

Man or Woman

Arrow, protection

Lightning and
Lightning Arrow:
swiftness, knowledge

Fire: heat, life,
the first element

It all happened long ago when the winter came and the animals had to creep into deep, deep holes to keep warm and safe. They grew very tired of having to sleep half the year. They were delighted one day to see lightning strike a tree and flames creep up the old dry trunk. They were determined to get some coals and keep a fire lit through the winter.

To get the coals, the animals had to cross water to the island where the tree was burning. Every animal that could swim or fly was eager to try to get a coal. The great raven, who was white in those days, was given the first chance. He was very strong. He flew over the water and landed on a branch high in the tree above the flames. While he was wondering what to do next, the smoke scorched all his feathers. He was so frightened that he flew back without a coal. He has been black ever since that day.

The screech owl had the next chance. When he landed on a high branch and peered down at the burning trunk, a blast of hot air nearly put his eyes out. For all his rubbing, he never could get the rings of feathers around his eyes to lay down flat again. This is why his eyes look so strange and he cannot see well in the daylight.

The screech owl returned without a coal. Two other birds tried and also failed. They asked the rabbit to try, but he turned white in terror. The fox said he couldn't swim. The cat refused to wet her paws.

The deer decided to give it a try. As he drew near the tree, his toes blistered, and he became frantic with pain and fear.

The reptiles had their turn next. First was the little blue racer. He swam across to the island and crawled to the tree. He climbed through a hole in the trunk, but the heat and smoke were too great for him. He lost his way and had a terrible time. By the time he got back, he was a shiny black.

When all the reptiles failed, the insects got their turn. They held a council and talked over whom they should send. They decided on the water spider. She could run on top of the water. She had no difficulty getting across to the island. To bring back the fire, she spun a web and fastened it tightly on her back. Into this web, she rolled a coal from the fire. She dragged her bundle to the water's edge and managed to float it over before the coal burned through the web.

Four who came to live on the waters and the land were Wazi, Owankanka, Anong Ite and Iktome.

Iktome tricked all the animals and the birds, but he feared Wazi and his old wife. Anong Ite feared Iktome because of her shame.

Iktome appeared as a very handsome man before the tipi of Anong Ite one day.

"Why do you come here?" Anong Ite asked.

"I am sorry for the misery I caused you."

"If only you could take me back to my people, then I would be happy again," Anong Ite cried.

Iktome left. When he returned, he had wild game for Anong Ite. She dried the meat and cured the skins. She made clothing with beautiful geometric designs. She packed everything into a bundle.

Iktome gave the bundle to the wolf. The wolf went into a cave, deep into the dark warm womb of Maka. The wolf saw the camps of people far, far away.

Although the wolf could see the people, he could not get to them until summer, autumn and winter had passed. Just before spring, he came face to face with one of the strong and brave men of the camp.

The man asked the wolf where he was going with his bundle.

"I am a friend of the people," said the wolf. "Iktome and Anong Ite have sent food and clothes."

The man told the wolf that his name was Tokahe, which means "the first man to have lived in a cave." Tokahe took the clothes and meat to his wife, Inawizi, who was an envious woman. She showed off all her new clothes and dried meat. Tokahe told the people that plenty of wild game for skins and meat could be found outside the cave. An old man suggested that three men go with Tokahe to see if he was telling the truth.

When the moon was full, they met the wolf, who led them back through the cave. When Anong Ite saw them coming, she was happy. She prepared a big feast for the men. Iktome invited them to eat soup and meat. Anong Ite covered the ugly side of her face. The men thought she was beautiful.

Iktome appeared as a very handsome man. He told the guests that he and his wife stayed young because they ate meat.

When the men had eaten their fill, Anong Ite gave them gifts and sent them home.

Iktome went with them to the entrance of the cave. He instructed the wolf to lead them back home. When the wolf returned from his trip, Iktome told him to wait at the entrance to the cave for the people who would be fooled by the stories of their leaders and would want to come out of the cave and onto the earth.

One of the old leaders of the people warned that those who left the cave would never again find the

entrance and would wander through cold, desolate mountains.

Tokahe and his wife persuaded six families to leave
with them. They met the wolf at the entrance to the cave.
He led them through a dark warm night to a strange
place. They became tired and hungry. Tokahe got sick.

Iktome appeared and laughed at their misery. Anong
Ite tried to comfort them, but they were terrified by the
ugly side of her face.

Then Wazi and Owankanka appeared to them and
gave them food and water and taught them how to sew
clothing. Wazi led them to the home of the water spider,
who ran across the water and fetched a burning coal for
them.

From that day on, these people were known as Peta
Oyate, the fire people, who lived alongside the water.

Ever since that day, a pregnant woman gathers fresh
twigs from the cottonwood tree. The twigs guard against
the pains of labor. Anong Ite delights in tormenting pregnant women with these pains. As further protection
against her, pregnant women make images of the lizard,
which is a symbol of endurance.

A long time ago, huge
chains of mountains formed all over the earth. One chain
of mountains resembled a snake. The Star Council People
gave it the name Mountains of the Serpents. This range is
now known as the Rocky Mountains.

It was here that the reptiles lived. These mountains
were surrounded with water in all directions. So the turtle
made its home there, too. The lizard could endure any-

thing. The turtle lived forever and ever. The snake always changed to a man and then back to a snake again.

The Peta Oyate moved to the Mountains of the Serpents and lived among the swift, flowing mountain streams. One day the whole camp was moving to the winter camp, but this one young girl, Anpa Wicahpi, fell in love with a man who always changed himself into a snake and lived high up in the caves of the Rocky Mountains.

The girl stayed behind and lived with the snake-man. Eventually, she became pregnant and had four oblong eggs. She was waiting for the precious eggs to hatch when a jealous man from her tribe came to find her. Hinhan Hota grabbed the four eggs and tossed them into the raging fire. The mother knelt down and tried to save her babies, but the shells broke and the tiny snakes lay helpless in the leaping flames. The flames burned and singed the mother's hair and face. And it was too late. The babies were already dead.

She wept bitterly and cursed Hinhan Hota.

The jealous man grabbed the woman and dragged her from her home. As they left, he stepped on a huge, shiny snake. He kicked the snake out of his way.

"Leave me here," pleaded the woman. "My husband, Wicasa Hanska, is home now."

The ugly jealous man forced her to go home with him. They followed the trail below the old home of the snake. Anpa Wicahpi turned and saw a flashing, shining object among the rocks. It was her husband, mourning his babies.

The woman arrived at her mother's camp very sick.

A man came to heal her and shook a rattle over the dying woman. The ritual lasted through the night. Toward dawn, her breathing became fainter and after awhile it slowly died away. Her hand still clutched a quilled turtle and a tiny sand lizard.

It was from this incident that the Peta Oyate changed their name to Zuzeca, meaning "snake."

The Zuzeca watched Mato Paha, a volcano, come into existence after a huge bear and the water monster, Unktehila, had a fight. Their blood flowed into the ravines and soaked the land. The injured bear climbed up to the top of the volcano and slept. Whenever the giant bear stirs in his sleep, the volcano trembles. Shale slides down the volcano's sides as the bear breathes.

Mato Paha is known today as Bear Butte.

The Chekpa Oyate, a nation of twins, live in the Mato Paha. They still hover over campsites, peeking in, looking for a place to be born. They always appear tied together with a rope.

The Oyate Teztela (Little People) used to live in the Mato Paha after the war of the bear and the water monster. These people were only twelve inches tall. They had mean tempers and were very strong. The Zuzeca were afraid of them. There were so many of the Oyate Teztela that when they attacked a full-sized man, they looked like a swarm of big red ants, climbing and biting. They soaked their arrowheads and the tips of their spears in rattlesnake venom.

The Zuzeca always left them strips of meat and other food crumbs.

One day the Oyate Teztela sent four men down the base of the volcano to give the Zuzeca their first skin-covered war shield. From then on, the two nations were allies.

The other volcano, Harney Peak, became the dwelling place of the dreaded bird. Although the Zuzeca had always lived on the lower fringes, they were careful not to disturb the bird. They knew an old story about how the ugly bird's outstretched wings could obscure the sky. The bird, they said, was a gigantic Indian who could put on wings and feathers as a man puts on a robe during the cold weather. Once costumed, he flies out in search of his prey. Little children are his favorite food. The outline of his great wings against the sky is jagged, like lightning. The beating of his wings is like thunder. He takes children who have wandered off or who have disobeyed. He tucks them into his ears and flies back to the volcano with them. Eventually, these missing children become new stars in the Milky Way.

One night, a little girl was disobedient. Her mother thought to scare her by saying, "*Heyankaka, le ichu,*" meaning, "Evil bird, take this girl away."

Suddenly, a huge claw reached down for the girl and clutched her away.

The evil bird put the girl in his ear and took her to the mountain. He beat her with the branch of a rose bush to keep her from escaping. He liked to keep her with him always, and he would tuck her into his ear when he went flying. Finally, she managed to get to the edge of his ear and fall out. She fell through a cloud and landed on the tip of a sharp rock, part of the Needles.

Her father searched for her for many years. One day,

he climbed some mountains and fasted for four days and nights, cleansing himself. On the last day he had a vision of his daughter sitting above him on pointed rocks. She told him she was happy. She said he didn't need to search for her any more.

This evil bird used swallows as messengers. Whenever people see swallows about, they gather up all their children and keep them inside.

To the north is Mato Tipila, or the Devil's Tower, a rock formation known to the Zuzeca as the home of the giant bears and their claws. This is how it was formed: One day several little girls wandered away from camp and got lost. Finally, from far away, searchers spotted the girls on a little mound. Bears were closing in on them.

From the clouds a voice spoke to the girls. "*Paha akilipo*. Climb up the hill," it commanded.

The earth shook as the small ridge began to rise out of the ground, carrying the children high into the air. The bears, left below, growled and clawed at the sides of the rising tower. Rocks poured down from the spire and scattered the bears. Huge birds rescued the girls and carried them back to their camp.

The Zuzeca learned from their ancestors that a strange man came into the camp one day. He wore fur clothing. His skin was white. He carried the symbol of the four directions with a wreath of sage hanging from it. He spoke in a different language. He pointed to the four directions, to the sun and to the earth. Then he walked away, never to be seen again. He had given the Zuzeca the Dance of the Swirling Suns. Only bold hunters, warriors, leaders, medicine men and holy people did the dance. Devil's Tower in Wyoming marked the spot of his coming. It became Winwanyag Wachipi Paha, or "Hill of the Sun Dance." This was the fourth ritual given to the people. The traditional sun dance takes place during the full moon every June.

Each year the Zuzeca returned to the water during the time of the great harvest moon. They set up camps in shade along the water. The cool breeze flowed through the open tipis. The young mothers and children learned to imitate the calls of different waterfowl as all the families were out harvesting wild rice.

It was during one of these harvests that a young mother fell out of her canoe into the deep, dark water. Her five-year-old son cried and called out to her, but she was gone. Sobbing, he paddled the canoe to shore and went to tell his father.

A year later, the boy and his father were back for the wild rice harvest. They paddled to the place where the boy's mother had drowned. When they reached the spot, she rose up out of the water. The boy could see that she was part fish; she had fins and scales from the waist down.

"I can never come home again," said the sad-faced woman. "I have another husband who is a giant gray fish."

The boy and his father never returned to the wild rice harvest.

All the creatures of the earth gathered once a year for a great race at the wild rice ponds. Iyapa, the camp crier, informed newcomers of the rules and kept the race going and all the creatures in order.

For the start of the race, all the birds rushed to their chosen spots. From the lakes, rivers and green marshes came the geese, the ducks, the gulls and all the birds that find their food in the earth's waters. Out of the black, dark forests emerged the vultures, the hawks, the owls, the crows and magpies. From the sandhills came the cranes whose loud calls resembled an Indian war cry. From the sandy banks of the shallow streams and from the rocky cliffs came the brilliant swallows, messengers of the clouds and storms. From the four winds, from every direction, came every sort of bird, each hoping to win the big race.

The four-legged creatures of the land all came, too, each lining up according to its size, with the larger and stronger animals in the rear.

The moon passed over the mountains, and the morning star appeared. When the starter shouted, *"Hokane! Hokane!" the race was on.*

Before the race was very old, many of the smaller, weaker creatures had been trampled or crushed. The dust from the pounding hooves rose into the sky and choked the swift flying creatures. The water creatures could not get out of the rice ponds.

Soon the string of racers stretched into a red ribbon of flesh, teeth, heads, fur and feathers. Millions of bones were left behind in the dust.

Mapiyato looked down in horror and anger. He shook the sky and set all the racing creatures spinning in it. Soon they were all part of a snake chasing its tail around the earth.

Still, they raced. They kept up the chase until the flames of a giant shooting star engulfed them and the ashes covered all their bodies and bones. Only those creatures hiding in deep, dark caves survived.

The Tiatuwan Oyate looked to the eastern sky, to the seven lights blinking below the crescent moon. They remembered that those seven stars in the Big Dipper were once their home. They began using one campfire to represent each tribe among them.

Tiatuwan means "lost and looking for their homes." These were the people who were swept away during a great flood. They had lived in the mountains, but when the flood waters receded, they found themselves on the prairies. They had been the Zuzeca Oyate before the flood. When they remembered their origin in the stars, they were able to reorient themselves and to give new names to each group among them.

Two brothers sitting in front of a campfire got into an argument. One picked up some ashes and flung them into his brother's face. These were the Olakota-speaking people known as Oglala.

Vision Seeking

Eagle Feather:
ceremonies, healing

Sun (*Wi*)

8 / THE SECOND WORLD INTERPRETED:

Two more great rituals unite seeker with spirit

Some of the Makaha's most important symbols and two of our great rituals come from the stories of the second world.

Tokahe is the first man, emerging from the womb of the earth onto its surface. He is without a soul. He learns from the Bison People how to find food, clothing and shelter on earth. His survival depends entirely on the bison.

The women with Tokahe begin to learn about the power of the cottonwood tree, one of the "standing people."

When you cut through an upper limb of the cottonwood tree and look at the grain of the wood, you will see a five-pointed star, a reminder of our souls' origin in the heavens.

The five points on the star in the cottonwood signify that once in every five generations a person will be given special powers, either the power to heal or the power to see.

The last person in my family to have possessed these special powers was Mary Standing Soldier, who had the power of the bear and was a healer. Medicine man Kenny Moses of the Sauk Suiattle tribe in the Pacific Northwest has told me that I am the next of my family, five generations after Mary Standing Soldier, to have the special powers. I am a seer, not a healer.

The cottonwood is the center of our sun dance ritual, the most fearsome and awe-inspiring of all our ceremonies, and one that originated in the stories of the second world.

The cottonwood tree has a connection to the Little People, those helpers from the stories of the second world. No one knows where the Little People came from before they lived at Bear Butte. The Makaha people always left them scraps of meat and tufts of duck down. The Little People, in return, tried to lead the Makaha to good hunting places. At night they stayed awake and listened to the coyotes yelp as they followed the buffalo herds. The next day the Little People would tell the Makaha which direction the coyotes and the buffalo were traveling.

One day the Little People were sitting in the leaves of a cottonwood tree. When the wind blew, the voices of the tree instructed the Little People how to fold the leaves to make a cone-shaped shelter. A Makaha elder was watching them and took back to his people the pattern for the tipi.

The Little People also taught my people how to make war shields. A war shield was the hide from the breast of the buffalo stretched over a frame of choke cherry branches. The choke cherry is a pliable tree, and its branches can be formed into a circle for the shield. The

Little People told the Makaha to decorate their war shields according to individual visions. This way the warrior had the power of the buffalo and the power of his vision to protect him from his enemies.

The stories of the second world tell us the origin of fire and show that the spider, who also is a trickster, has a side that is beneficial to humans. The spider's industrious and clever nature balances his deviousness.

From these stories, we get the lizard as a symbol of endurance. Because the lizard could change colors, it was hard to spot, thus hard to kill. My ancestors believed that the lizard was a decoy for evil spirits, luring them away from infants. This is why Anpa Wicahpi was clutching a tiny sand lizard when she died. She was still hoping for the protection of her babies.

Anpa Wicahpi died clutching a turtle, too. This creature signifies strength, long life and the power to survive. A turtle heart keeps on beating long after the turtle is dead. The slow pace of the turtle allows it to study everything it passes. This gives it spiritual insight.

The story of Anpa Wicahpi's marriage to the snakeman was a reminder to my people of their origin in the Rocky Mountains and their leaving of that place. The snake is often equated with the rainbow and is the guardian of all that grows.

The different names given to the people describe their changing circumstances and surroundings. Going from the Fire People (Peta Oyate) to the Snake People (Zuzeca Oyate) to the People Looking for a Home (Tiatuwan Oyate), they eventually settled into seven tribes, or the seven campfires (Ocheti Shakowin).

The Oglala lived beneath two volcanoes. They take their name from the ashes that one volcano flung on the other. Oglala means the scattering of ashes. My people, the Makaha, are a band of the Oglala tribe.

The other six tribes or campfires of the Olakota-speaking Sioux are the Itazipcho (Without Bows), the Minneconjou (Plant Beside the Stream), the Sihasapa (Black Feet), the Sichangu (Burned Thighs), the Hunkpapa (At the Camping Circle Entrance, or Buffalo Gap) and the Ooenunpa (Two Boiling Kettles).

The stories of the second world reflect so much of the landscape in which my ancestors made their home. Where the stories of the first world are concerned primarily with celestial events, the stories of the second world tell of great geological happenings. The story of the wild rice pond reflects the fact that much of the area where my ancestors lived was at one time under water. That's why mermaids are part of the lore of South Dakota.

The story about the great race among all the animals is one tale in which heaven and earth collide. I interpret this story as the recounting of a time when a giant meteorite crashed into earth, blocking the sun with its huge fiery cloud and killing most of the creatures living at that time.

The man looking for his lost daughter, taken from him by the bird beast, is the first vision seeker of my people. Crying for a vision, *hanblecheyapi*, is one of the seven great rituals. It is often performed today, but much of its purity has been lost.

There are many reasons to go vision seeking, one of which is to prepare for the great and solemn sun dance ritual. A person who wants a better understanding of her place in the universe and her oneness with all things will undertake the four-day and four-night fast. Other vision seekers are those who want a favor from Wakan Tanka or those who would give thanks for a favor already granted.

No one should go vision seeking without rigorous preparation, which includes both physical and spiritual cleansing. I recommend a year's preparation, particularly if the vision seeking is going to be followed by the sun dance.

The vision seeker first must consult a medicine man who will act as adviser and interpreter of whatever vision is received.

Then the vision seeker must begin purification, going to sweat lodges as often as possible, undertaking daylong fasts to condition the body. These fasts should be accompanied by praying and singing and should be conducted in solitude.

Only those who are well prepared to enter the realm of the Great Mystery will be rewarded with the gift of its powers.

The medicine man suggests the vision seeking site. He will pray over the matter, and the right site will come to him. Men go to mountaintops. Women do their vision seeking on the lower slopes. This is according to the old ways, which were more protective of women lest they be snatched from their solitude by a rival tribe.

A woman who is ready for her time in the wilderness selects another woman to go with her. This companion will stand away, far enough to insure the vision seeker's solitude but near enough to hear her cries for assistance.

A man takes a male companion with him for the same purpose.

The medicine man will sit in a sweat lodge for the four days and four nights of the vision seeker's quest, fasting and praying just as the seeker is.

Setting out for the site, the woman is simply dressed, perhaps in a cotton garment. She is unadorned and barefoot. She carries only a shawl, on which she will sit or with which she can wrap herself against the cold.

A man also keeps his dress plain. He is casting off the material world and begging for entry into the spiritual.

The medicine man has prepared five sticks for the quest. These are cottonwood saplings, cut to a length of four feet and stripped of their bark. When she arrives at the place of her vigil, the seeker will plant one of the sticks in the earth and will tie a string that is her height to it. Then she will take the loose end of the string, pull it taut and use it as the radius for the circle she walks and marks. This will be her sacred and protective circle. She will not leave it for four days and four nights.

She plants each of the other four sticks at each of the four directions on the perimeter of the circle. She ties her bag of tobacco on the center pole, for she will be sending prayers on the smoke of her pipe. She also fastens a spotted eagle feather, symbol of vision, to the center pole. Then she lines her circle with sage.

This sage will be her bed. It will also keep the circle clean of her bodily wastes. The woman who is the seeker's guardian comes when necessary to take the soiled sage away.

The seeker fills her pipe and places it in a specially prepared forked stick rack at the base of the pole marking the east. She goes to the pole marking the west and sits by it, facing east, facing her pipe.

She prays and sings. She concentrates always on that pole that is in the center, for Wakan Tanka is the center of all things. She prays for all her relatives and all her friends. She thinks back over her life. She empties herself so that she will feel the new direction when it comes.

The seeker can walk around, lie down, sit, stand up, do anything she wants as long as she does not leave the circle. This is for her protection. Evil spirits will come, but they will not step inside the circle. When they do begin to taunt her, the seeker can light her pipe and pray them away. Or she can burn sweet grass or sage, and the smoke will defend her.

The evil spirits standing outside the circle, encouraging the seeker to end her four-day and four-night vigil prematurely, usually take the form of people. Sometimes they are very beautiful people. Sometimes the seeker has to use all of her strength to resist them. She must hang on to her pipe and realize that she has vowed to keep her solitary watch for four days and four nights.

I have a friend who left after three days because women kept appearing to him, tempting him to come out of his circle. Finally, he gave in.

The seeker must be focused, single-minded and strong.

A woman I know did keep her fast. She stayed for the four days and four nights even though she kept hearing her mother cry. She discovered when she came down from the hillside that her father had died. Her family had not wanted to bring her down, so they waited until her vigil was over to tell her.

The seeker must be alert to everything that happens while she is in the circle and must remember it so that she can take it all back to the medicine man for his interpretation. She must pay attention to all the animals that appear to her, even the most seemingly insignificant ant. If she sleeps, she must note her dreams.

My cousin Russell Means said the only thing that came to him during his vision quest was a big black fly. He was not sure what that meant. If the quest is inconclusive, the seeker can return.

The seeker's adviser, sitting in the sweat lodge, is going through the same things. The two people, the seeker and the adviser, are of one mind. The medicine man, who has gotten his powers from repeated vision quests, can usually find an explanation for what has happened to the seeker during her vigil.

The seeker will spend much of her time in battles

with the evil spirits. But there is a time during the last day or last night that things become very calm. This is the time when the seeker may have a vision. She may see a future event for which she has to prepare. She may know that her favor has been granted.

I am planning my next vision quest as preparation for a sun dance, during which I will give thanks to the creator for healing my son Melvin after a terrible fall that should have been fatal. Since I'm going up there because of Melvin, I may have a vision of his full future life. I may be allowed to understand why he did live, what plans there are for him that made the extension of his life possible against daunting odds.

When the four days and four nights come to an end, the seeker leaves her circle and goes down to the sweat lodge to recount her experience to the medicine man and to finish the ritual. Then there is much rejoicing of family and friends, who have been waiting for the seeker's return.

If a person has done vision seeking in preparation for the sun dance, then her regimen of cleansing and purification must continue until the day of that solemn ceremony.

The sun dance, *wiwanyag wachipi*, is a dance of thanksgiving. When times were darkest for Melvin's recovery, I committed myself to doing a sun dance in return for his life. If you ask a lot, you have to give a lot of yourself also. Once you commit yourself, you must participate in one sun dance a year for four years.

The sun dance is the only one of our great rituals that is entirely a dance. It takes place in the summertime. In the old days, the sun dance month was June. Now, on the Pine Ridge Reservation, sun dances are always in August, during the full moon. The dance lasts for four days and four nights.

Individual dancers prepare for this rite by continuing their prayer and attendance at sweat lodges. Anyone who would be a sun dancer must go vision seeking first. Oftentimes the vision will speak to how the sun dance is to be performed.

A long time ago people went vision seeking in June and then waited another year, until the next June, to go into the sun dance. Now most go vision seeking in June and go to the sun dance ceremony in August.

All thirty-seven tribes of the Plains Indians count the sun dance among their great rituals. However, very few actually hold sun dance ceremonies. On the Pine Ridge Reservation, five sun dances are held every August.

I will go to the sun dance at Wounded Knee.

There was a time during which the Bureau of Indian Affairs sought to make money from the traditional sun dance. Bureaucrats put on a rodeo and carnival in conjunction with the solemn ritual and sold tickets. Often as many as ten thousand people would attend those commercialized affairs.

Now the ceremonies have been returned to the care of those who understand their sacred nature. They are more private affairs, just the dancers and their families and friends. The size of the crowd is usually about three hundred.

A sun dancer should not engage in sex for the entire year before he or she dances. The dancer's training regimen includes getting up at sunrise and praying to the four directions every morning. The would-be dancer should spend a great deal of time alone the year before the dance, meditating.

During this year of preparation, the dancer should pay close attention to the phases of the moon and during the week before the full moon should burn a lot of sage and sweet grass. This is the week that souls tend to travel.

This is when they will be drawn to anyone needing advice.

The setting for the sun dance is a huge open field. A cottonwood tree is the center of the site. This tree is selected with great care. A tobacco offering is made to the tree before it is felled. Specially chosen people take one swing each with the ax until the tree is ready to topple. Four virgin women must witness the tree's fall. The trunk of the tree, including the part where the branches begin to fork, is not allowed to touch the ground. After its branches are trimmed off, the tree is carried to the hole that has been prepared for it in the center of the ceremonial site.

Before the tree is lifted into place, each dancer ties his or her flag to the top of it. These flags are four streamers—red, yellow, black and white—fastened to a stick. Each participant has to make one. If someone is absent from the dance one year before he has completed his four dances, his flag goes up anyway, awaiting his return.

Also attached to the cottonwood are one rawhide rope for each dancer, a figure of a man, a figure of a buffalo, and a small cherry tree, representing the hope that the people will be fruitful.

Long ago, when only one or two warriors would participate, the sun dance was in a lodge built of twenty-eight forked poles placed in a circle around the sacred cottonwood. Twenty-eight more poles ran from the fork of each post to the top of the cottonwood.

Twenty-eight is a sacred number because it is two sacred numbers multiplied: four and seven. It is also the number of ribs a buffalo has and the number of feathers in a war bonnet. Twenty-eight is the number of days in the complete lunar cycle. Each of those days has a meaning. Two are for the Great Mystery, Wakan Tanka. Two are for Maka, Mother Earth. Four are for the north, south, east and west winds. One is for the spotted eagle. One is for the sun, one for the moon and one for the morning star. Four are for the rock, fire, bow and pipe ages. Seven are for the seven great rituals. One is for the buffalo. One is for the fire, one for the water and one for the rock. And the last one is for the people, Ikche-Wichasha, the Real Natural Human Beings.

These days the sun dance has so many participants that a dance lodge is not built. A large open circle around the cottonwood is consecrated to the dance. The dancers prepare themselves in sweat lodges. They go once a day for four days prior to the dance.

On the morning of the sun dance, the dancers enter the sweat lodge on the sun dance grounds at 3 A.M. There may be several sweat lodges on the dance grounds, depending on the number of dancers. A sweat lodge can accommodate a maximum of fifteen people. If there are seventy-five dancers, there will be five sweat lodges.

The purification of the sweat lodge must be completed before the sun rises. The dancers must be in the circle around the cottonwood ready and waiting for the sun to rise.

Male dancers wear a red or blue cloth around their waists and rabbit fur around the ankles. The rabbit is a symbol of humility, and the dancer wants, above all, to express his humility in the face of the Great Mystery. We believe that humility is too profound for the creator to have given it to any creature fully. Humility is the awareness that any power we have is by the grace of the creator. Humility also believes that every human being has something to teach; although the human form is limited, the limitations are never the same from one person to the next. Female dancers wear the humble rabbit's fur on their ankles, too.

Women dance in a dark cotton dress. Some will wrap a shawl around their waists.

All dancers wear crowns of either sunflowers or sage. They are all barefooted. The men carry flutes made from the wing bones of eagles. Attached to each flute is a white plume from the breast of the spotted eagle.

All dancers file into the circle clockwise. As soon as the sun appears, the drum begins and the song is sung. This is a special sun dance song. It is a plea for strength and mercy, for endurance of this awesome undertaking.

Dancers move around the circle with their hands raised and their faces toward the sun. They dance this way for an hour. Then they rest for ten minutes. If thirsty, they drink choke cherry juice. They can move into the shade area that has been set up around the edge of the ceremonial site. This is where the spectators sit. It is a circle made of pine poles and roofed with pine branches.

The dance continues this way until the sun sets. When night comes, the dancers sleep on ground that has been covered with sage. Relatives cover them with blankets if the air is cool.

The sun dance lasts for four days and four nights. Dancers do not eat. As they whirl around the circle, they are trying to separate their spirits from their bodies, to send their *tonwan*s in a spiral to the heavens.

Friends or relatives of the dancers participate in the ritual by offering their flesh. They can give up to thirty pieces as a sign of their support for the dancers' aims and thankfulness to the creator.

The medicine man who is conducting the dance uses a razor blade to slice strips of flesh from the donors' shoulders or upper arms. These flesh offerings are wrapped in buckskin and taken to the sun dance pole.

The medicine man also works with dancers who have had visions about how they should participate in the sun dance. Some have had visions of pulling buffalo skulls around with them. The medicine man helps them attach the skulls. He ties a rawhide rope to each skull. He ties the other end of that rope to a sharpened skewer. Then he cuts the flesh on the dancer's back and threads the rope through it.

I've seen one man pulling thirteen skulls. The dancer whirls until they all fall off. If they have not fallen off by the end of the fourth day, all the children in the crowd will come and sit on these buffalo skulls until they break away from the dancer's back.

My grandmother's uncle had a vision that he was to have eagle feathers sewn to his arms like fringe for his sun dance. He was a glorious sight, raising his feathered arms to the sun as he whirled around the circle.

Dancers who offer themselves up to their visions in this way believe they are gaining strength. Their flesh is weak, but by enduring physical tests, they gain spiritual strength. There is a palpable sense of joy at these sun dance ceremonies. The dancers have the ecstasy of union with the Great Mystery. They take the spirits of the spectators with them.

On the fourth day, every dancer is attached to a piece of rawhide rope tied to the cottonwood pole. The medicine man draws the sharpened skewer at the dancer's end of the rope through a strip of flesh on the male dancers' chests and on the female dancers' upper arms. Once the rope is attached to a dancer, all his relatives and friends have to dance behind him until he breaks free. Once he is free, the dance is over for him. When everyone has broken free, there is a huge feast and much celebration.

Morning Star

Stone Boy

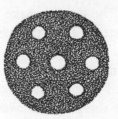

Rituals, Ceremonies

9 / CREATION STORIES FROM THE THIRD WORLD:

A healer turns hurtful

Creation stories from the third world comment on both human and geologic events. Stone Boy is the first human with healing powers, and he uses them to restore life to his tribe. In the process he gives his people what is to become their most basic ceremony, inipi, *or that of the sweat lodge. Unfortunately, Stone Boy is all too human and soon abuses his miraculous powers. His misguided actions touch off catastrophes, first a battering glacier, then a great flood. The people who survive are descended from the match between an eagle and a woman. They discover the pipe as an instrument of prayer, and they begin trying to recover the powers that Stone Boy squandered. The Makaha have a visual reminder of Stone Boy in the huge granite dome that covers much of the Paha Sapa, or Black Hills.*

Long ago a girl had ten brothers who were great hunters and warriors. One morning all of them came back from the forest except for the oldest, Chaske. The girl, Wi Tokape, was overwhelmed with worry. The second brother, Hepan, went looking for Chaske. Hepan did not return. All ten brothers disappeared in this way. Wi Tokape wandered everywhere, crying and shouting her brothers' names but finding not a trace of them.

She stopped to rest along a stream. It made little chuckling noises. She listened closely and looked at the pebbles on the bottom. One of those pebbles, she was sure, was making the noises. She fished it out of the water and slipped it into a leather pouch, which she strung from her neck. The tiny chuckles made her laugh and laugh, and she didn't feel so lonely any more.

She slept well that night. When she woke at dawn, she found a cuddly, very heavy baby boy on her chest. She loved and cared for him. She named him Stone Boy.

He was always too large for her to carry. He walked sooner than a normal baby. He learned how to use a bow and arrows and quickly became a great hunter.

One day he announced that he was going to look for his uncles' bones.

His mother begged him not to. She feared he would disappear the way his uncles had. "My grief would be too much to bear," she said.

Stone Boy promised not to get lost. He told his mother she would know he was alive as long as his pillow did not move.

She packed his food and moccasins and sadly watched him leave.

As he journeyed through the forest, he questioned every animal he met. At one point, he saw on the ground in front of him a severed finger. He stooped to pick it up. It looked like the smallest finger on a man's hand. He put it in his pouch.

Then he came to a fallen log, which had been struck by lightning. The ground around it bore the marks of a great struggle. Stone Boy found a bow there.

As he was fitting one of his arrows to the bow, a giant bird engulfed him and tried to carry him off. Stone Boy was too heavy, and soon the bird gave up, exhausted. It fell, a heap of feathers, beside him.

Stone Boy wondered whether the bird had taken his uncles. He pulled some scarlet down from the monster's head. As he held tight to the feathers, he felt them lift him. Soon he was high in the sky.

He landed in the country of the Thunderhead Mountains. He noticed the nest of a thunderbird. As he inspected the eggs in the nest, people came running toward him and shouting. He threw an egg at them. They all stopped and began to cry, "Give me my heart! Give me my heart!"

Stone Boy realized the hearts of the people were in the thunderbird eggs. He emptied the nest and returned the hearts to the people. Four eggs remained. Stone Boy took those with him as he resumed his journey.

He found four little boys who agreed to take him to his uncles' bones. When they got to a large mound in the woods, he asked the boys to bring water, wood, stones and slender willow branches. He would build an *inipi*, a sweat lodge.

He bent the willow sticks into a domed frame, which he covered with buffalo robes. Outside he built a fire and set rocks in it to heat.

As he poured water on the hot stones, a voice came from the steam. Then more voices, shouting. He pulled open the flap of the sweat lodge, and out came his ten uncles, intact except for their hearts and the little finger of the youngest uncle. He broke open the eggs and gave his uncles their hearts. He gave his youngest uncle his little finger.

For a long while, Stone Boy, his mother and uncles all lived a happy life. Then Stone Boy began killing animals and taking only their hearts, teeth and claws while mocking them. Wi Tokape and her brothers begged him to show respect for the sacred animals.

Stone Boy told his mother that the animals planned to wage war on them. He said he had heard a bison shouting the war cry. He had also heard the beaver and muskrat ask the swallow to fly to the home of Wakinyan, the great giant of the west.

"What will Wakinyan do to us?" asked Wi Tokape.

"Wakinyan's wife will shake out her feathers while Wakinyan blows them in our direction."

Stone Boy picked up five pebbles and threw them into the air. When they landed, they created a stone wall around the tipi. With a sixth and seventh pebble, he built two stone tipis, one on top of the other. He informed his mother and his uncles that he would defend the camp alone.

When the animals attacked, they swarmed in hundreds. They were all the creatures, big and tiny, bird and beast. They could not get to Stone Boy, and he killed them by the thousands.

The swallow told Wakinyan of the slaughter. He grew angry and sent rain in torrents. The rain turned to sleet, then into a blinding snow storm. The snowflakes turned to pellets.

Stone Boy retreated into his tipi. His mother and uncles were already cowering there.

Debris-filled ice struck at the fortress in sheets. Then water came pouring in through the holes the badgers, gophers and moles had dug. Stone Boy's mother and his uncles drowned in the muddy water.

He survived but was half-buried in the earth. You can see him still in the Paha Sapa.

The Oglala discovered Stone Boy after the great flood. During this flood, the water got so high that people started floating away. Nations were destroyed.

As the waters rose, a young girl tried desperately to stay above them. She climbed a tall tree high upon a mountain. An old spotted eagle saw her and told her to hop onto his back. They flew to dry land. She became the eagle's wife and bore twins. These twins, a boy and a girl, became the ancestors of the great eagle nation.

When the muddy waters went down, the people found themselves on the "Hills of the Prairies." They drew together and mourned their dead. The blood of the dead had formed a giant red stone —the pipestone.

Then Tunkasila, a thoughtful man, took the red dirt from beneath the earth in his hands and fashioned a pipe. He offered the pipe to the east, then the south, west and north. The smoke wafted over all the people as a symbol of peace.

One evening two maidens were watching the sky for a certain twinkling star. "I love that bright star," said the first maiden. "If it were a man, I would marry him and go away."

The other maiden laughed out loud at that.

As she guffawed, the twinkling star fell from the sky

and crashed into the earth. When the dust cleared, a young man stood before the two maidens.

"I have come to marry you," said the star-man, "and to take you to my home in the sky."

The second girl ran in fright. The first one nodded yes and followed the star-man to his home. They lived there happily, and the woman was with child.

"When you go to dig wild turnips, do not press your turnip digger too hard into the earth," the star-man advised her.

The woman's body was so heavy that when she pressed on her turnip digger, the earth opened up and she fell through and was killed. Her baby boy, however, was unhurt, crying and kicking as he fell. A hawk flying by snatched him out of the air and took him to all the other winged creatures. They all asked the eagle who should care for the child. The meadowlark volunteered.

"We have a large family and we are very poor, but we will take the boy and raise him and call him Star Boy," the meadowlark said.

Star Boy grew into a fine man. He eventually returned to his father's home.

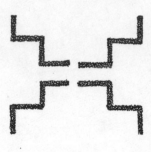

Water

Sweat Lodge

10 / THE THIRD WORLD INTERPRETED:

The essential ritual cleanses the people

Creation stories from the third world name Pipestone, Minnesota, as a sacred place. This site near the South Dakota border is the only source in the world for the claylike earth from which we make our ceremonial red pipes. Veins of pipestone run beneath outcroppings of quartzite. Only a few people have permits to dig the pipestone, which is easy to carve, like a piece of cedar.

The pipe is the link between a person and Wakan Tanka. On every puff of smoke, we send a prayer. The pipe is the one object that we use in every ceremony.

In the last series of creation stories, those from the fourth world, the White Buffalo Calf Woman brings specific instructions about ceremonial use of the pipe. Before her appearance, however, people used pipes to sanctify and to seal promises. Nearly every family had a pipe that was a prized possession, one to be shared with others but never borrowed. To this day, a pipe is the most significant possession a Makaha can inherit.

My family has four pipes, each more than two hundred years old. My personal pipe is red, made of pipestone. The bowl is about two inches in diameter. I carry it and its ash stem in a pouch, and I assemble the pipe for my own rituals. For instance, at the changing of the moon, when it becomes full, at midnight I always pray with my little pipe. I gave a similar little red pipe to my son James for use in his personal rituals. I felt he needed it when he first went vision seeking in 1983.

We also have a black pipe, the same size as the two little red ones. Black pipes are used for healing. I've never used my black pipe because I am not a healer. I gave the pipe to my son Richard since he's studying to be a medical doctor. He hasn't used it yet. Maybe in time he will.

The fourth family pipe now belongs to my youngest, Melvin. It is a larger pipe, about four inches in diameter. I gave it to Melvin because he began his sun dance ritual at the age of fourteen. He uses it all the time. He takes it to every sweat lodge we go to, and he passes it around at the end. Many people don't own pipes, so we share ours.

The type of pipe that has passed into Caucasian consciousness is the peace pipe. My people were sincere in their desire for peace. If a peace pipe was brought to Oglala warriors in the thick of battle, they would drop their weapons to smoke. They believed that if they refused the pipe, they would suffer disaster. In fact, our history contains several examples of warriors who refused the pipe and then died ingloriously.

The peace that my people prayed for with the pipe was peace without slavery. Such a conditional peace was apparently not what the whites wanted.

A pipe is the herald of the sweat lodge ceremony. To ask a person to conduct a sweat lodge, you take him a pipe. If he smokes your pipe, he agrees to build a lodge and perform the ceremony.

The sweat lodge is our basic ceremony, one we must perform before we attempt any other ritual. This is because we, like Stone Boy, have abused the powers made available to us by the Great Mystery. We have behaved without respect and been too caught up in our own small accomplishments and problems to let the universe flow through us.

Before he developed power sickness, Stone Boy taught us how to heal and to restore life. His story leaves us both the instructions for *inipi* and the example of what will happen if we forget the humility inherent in that rite.

The sweat lodge is first of all a cleansing for every individual who participates. You have to heal yourself before you can heal anyone else.

An architectural symbol of transformation, the sweat lodge is framed with sixteen willow sticks bent to form a circular wall with a domed roof. The person performing the ceremony prays and makes tobacco offerings to the trees he cuts. He usually recruits about twenty people to help him prepare the willow frame and perform other duties necessary during the ceremony.

Their first task is to select a quiet site. About ten paces from where they will erect the lodge, to the east, they construct a sacred fireplace. This is where the rocks will be heated. My ancestors carried a coal from camp to camp so that the same fire always heated the rocks. The fire represents the eternal spirit. Nowadays, we build each fire anew, placing four sticks running east and west and on top of them four sticks running north and south, and surrounding the square with four standing sticks, as in a tipi.

After praying and lighting the fire, the leader goes to the center of the circle that will be the lodge and digs a hole. This will be the sacred pit to which the heated rocks are brought during the ceremony. The leader and his helpers carry the dirt from this hole east out of the circle about twelve feet from the lodge, just beyond the fire. There they build a small mound, which represents Grandmother Earth. Any offerings—sage, sweet grass, cedar—that people want to make can go in or on the grandmother mound.

Once the willow frame is up, the leader hangs an eagle feather from the center of the dome. Then he and his assistants cover the frame with tarps, blankets and quilts, tied on with ropes. A long time ago, people used buffalo robes.

One piece of material at the east is left as a flap so that people can come and go. The ground inside is covered with sage.

The sweat lodge always faces east out of reverence for the star-man, who is Venus, visible in the eastern sky before daybreak. East is also the direction from which the light of wisdom comes. Opening the flap admits wisdom.

Once the lodge with its pit, the sacred fire and the grandmother mound are all in place, the leader fills the ceremonial pipe and takes it into the lodge with him. He walks clockwise around the wall until he reaches the west. There he burns sweet grass and purifies himself, the pipe and the entire lodge in its fragrant smoke.

When the first purification ritual is complete, he walks out of the lodge and leans the pipe against the grandmother mound, with the bowl on the west side and the stem slanting to the east.

Meanwhile, granite river stones the size of softballs have been heating in the fire. They are red-hot, so close to being pure energy that you can almost see through them. Usually, there are seven stones on the fire for each of the four rounds of the ritual, making twenty-eight stones used altogether.

The sweat lodge ceremony is performed at sundown. To get started, the leader enters the lodge and walks clockwise all the way around until he is nearly back to where he began. He sits cross-legged near the door. Other participants follow him in, sitting one after another until they have filled the semicircle that ends at the westernmost point of the structure. This is the place where the guest of honor will sit. The honored one walks in, carrying the gourd rattles that will be a rhythmic accompaniment to the songs and prayers offered. He sits, and the remaining places fill up.

My ancestors held small sweat lodge ceremonies, usually with no more than four participants. These days as many as fifteen fill the tiny hut. Everyone sits cross-legged facing the center.

The fire tender brings in the hot stones one at a time, balancing each in the fork of a stick. When the pit is filled with stones, the fire tender closes the flap so that the lodge is dark except for the red glow from the pit.

Prayers begin. During the first round, we usually pray for all the people who made the sweat lodge possible. Participants sprinkle sage, sweet grass and cedar over the rocks in the pit. Everybody has brought a bit of this incense.

The leader pours water on the stones. As the aromatic steam rises, the person on the leader's left is the first to pray or sing. She holds a drum and strikes it as she gives voice to whatever is on her mind. Participants in the sweat lodge ceremony can talk about whatever they want for as long as they want. They end with the phrase, "all my relatives," and pass the drum to the next person.

When the drum has made its way around to the leader and everyone has had a turn at chanting or singing, the first round is over. The flap opens, and anyone wishing to leave can.

The fire tender brings in a new load of stones, and the whole process begins again.

During the first round, people have begun to relax. When they go into the sweat lodge, they are usually tense, overwhelmed with their own emotions. As the steam escapes when the flap finally opens, the anxiety of the participants rushes out with it.

During the first round, I try to concentrate on the rhythm of the drum and rattles, the quality of people's voices and the fragrance of the steam. By the second round, I'm ready to pay attention to the way the heat touches my body and the way the drum feels in my hands. Often during this round, I ask my loved ones who are deceased to touch me. I have felt their pats on my shoulders and legs.

The third round is a repeat of the first two. This is when I try to concentrate on the sense of sight. I watch the flames leap as people put their offerings on the red-hot rocks. I feel my eyes lose their focus in the glow of the stones. If I am open and relaxed, I can move from sight to vision.

The most beautiful sweat lodge vision I had began as a gold spiral of light, which coalesced into a sun. When I turned my head to the left, I saw the faces of thousands and thousands of Indian people. When I turned to the right, I saw thousands more faces, like masks.

It is during the third round that I begin to feel the power of the circle. Its pull is very strong. This is the cohesion of the healing energy.

If you see skeletons during a sweat lodge ceremony, you are having a positive vision. The skeletons are powerful healers. We call their medicine ghost healing. When a skeleton adjusts its bones and sits down between two flesh-and-blood people in a sweat lodge, the power of the circle surges.

The fourth round is a repeat of the first three. It ends with the passing of the pipe. After everyone has smoked, the sweat lodge ceremony is over. People emerge from the hut cleansed and refreshed.

For me, the sweat lodge has been an important part of life since I was five and allowed to enter the one my grandparents, Theresa and Theodore Means, kept outside their house in Wounded Knee. My grandparents used their sweat lodge every night. Visitors would arrive and would go out into the sweat lodge with my grandfather.

Before I was permitted to participate in the ceremony, I was very curious about the inside of that hut. I was forbidden to enter it, but I often circled it and got as close to it as I could without going in. Once when I was tempted to lift the flap and go in, I suddenly heard voices singing from inside the lodge. I knew no one of human acquaintance was in there. My curiosity cooled for a while.

Many years later, a different kind of voice coming from within a sweat lodge had a soothing, rather than a startling, effect on me. When my husband died, the man who performed his burial ceremonies told me I would hear his voice again after he had been dead for a year. I did not doubt this prediction. I wondered what he would say to me and how he would sound.

The night before his memorial dinner, which we gave on the year's anniversary of his death, my brother Leonard began building a sweat lodge down by the creek, quite a way from the house. He quit for the night just as he was ready to cover the frame.

The next morning, as my other brother Robert and I were in the house making more preparations, we heard the sound of a drum coming from the direction of the sweat lodge. I looked at Robert and said, "Do you hear what I hear?" And he said, "If you're hearing the drum, that's what I'm hearing."

We stopped our work and walked toward the sweat

lodge. We heard the sound more clearly as we approached the willow frame. We stood outside the sticks and listened to the gentle drumming coming from their center. We saw nothing, neither a drummer nor a drum. The sound, however, was unmistakable.

I was overcome by a feeling of peace. I realized I had been dreading hearing from my husband on the anniversary of his death. I had expected to hear a human voice, and I had thought maybe he would call my name. I had wondered how I would react to the call of that dear voice.

His speaking to me with the voice of a drum, however, calmed me. I felt his rhythmic tranquility in the other world. I felt his steady heart pulsing in time with the universe.

When I moved to the Pacific Northwest from Wounded Knee, I knew no one qualified to lead the sweat lodge ceremony. If I wanted to participate in the cleansing ritual, I had to travel home to South Dakota.

Then one day at a pow wow in Seattle, I met a Chippewa man named Bob Shimek. He was just beginning to learn the songs of his tribe and to sing them at pow wows. I started to see him often. Every time I looked at his face, I noticed a white mist passing over it.

I told him about the mist, and he said that for his tribe, white is a symbol of death. I was sure I was seeing something other than death, but I did not know what it was.

Finally, when he was singing at another pow wow, the mist revealed itself. It solidified into a buffalo skull covering his head and shoulders. I was too shocked to say anything to him at the time. I was surprised to see the symbol of my people mounted on the body of a Chippewa.

By the next day I had recovered enough to go to Bob's office to tell him what I had seen and to puzzle over its meaning with him. That's when he told me about a bone he had been carrying. He said he had been walking in St. Louis one day when an old man stopped him and said he wanted to give him a very powerful old bone.

We had that bone analyzed, and we discovered it had been part of a bison.

After that revelation, Bob realized his obligation to pass on the power of that bone. He apprenticed himself to a Chippewa in Minnesota named Jim Eagle, and he learned how to set up the morning star sweat lodge and conduct the ceremony.

Now whenever anyone in the Seattle area needs a sweat lodge, Bob Shimek sets one up.

Bob's sweat lodges have been a salvation for me. In fact, it was those sweat lodges that kept me and my entire family going when Melvin had a construction accident in September of 1987. He was putting a new roof on a three-story apartment building when he leaned on a parapet that gave way. He plunged feet first until he hit a tree that flipped him over so that he met the concrete sidewalk head-on.

I was in Wounded Knee at the time, but I knew something was wrong. As I picked cherries, I kept smelling sweet grass. Eventually I heard someone walk up behind me. I didn't even turn around. I just said, "What have you come to tell me this time?"

I got my answer when I arrived back at my grandmother's house and heard the news of Melvin's accident.

The first thing I did was burn sage and sweet grass. I had Melvin's pipe with me. I don't know why. But I filled it, and we smoked the pipe and had great faith in the prayers we were sending.

Melvin was in a coma for seventeen days, and during that time his *nagi* would not leave us alone. Our belief is that when a person is in a coma, his soul really roams.

My son Richard would be trying to sleep, and someone would tap him on the shoulder or pat him on the head. As I lay in my bed, I felt fingers pinching me. The radio that Melvin kept in the bathroom would blast to life, even after we had unplugged it.

The only thing that kept us sane during this time was the sweat lodge.

When Melvin developed pneumonia, I asked the medicine man Kenny Moses of the Sauk Suiattle tribe to perform a healing ceremony at the hospital. While he was chanting and waving his arms over Melvin, I heard someone crying beside me. I looked over and saw a girl dressed in white lace with ruffles at the waist. Her long black hair streamed down over her face. As I stared, she faded into Melvin's bed.

Kenny told me later that she was one of Melvin's great-great-grandmothers. She had pulled a tipi over the whole bed, he said. She wanted Melvin to live because she had plans for him.

Melvin came out of his coma two days after the healing ceremony. He had to stay in the hospital for another month. When he came home, he was very weak and had no flesh on him. His eyes and his bones were huge.

Now he is back to his normal 185 pounds, and I am preparing myself for the sun dance to give thanks for his recovery.

I am also working with the United Indians of All Tribes to introduce children of alcoholics to the healing powers of the sweat lodge. Most of these people are so numb that they are not even aware of their physical senses. By adapting the talking circle that is the basic form of the sweat lodge ceremony, I can help children of alcoholics begin their own recovery.

I seat the group in a circle and I pass around water first, telling the story about how Iyan created Maka and gave her five gifts, which are the physical senses. I ask each one in the circle to take a sip of water and to concentrate on how it tastes. I pass around sage and sweet grass. I talk about the sense of smell. We release the fragrance of each bundle with fire. Next I pass around the eagle feather, the sense of sight, and then the drum, representing hearing. As each person handles each object going around the circle, I try to call attention to the feel of the thing and to reawaken the sense of touch.

This little ritual takes at least an hour. As they touch each object, the people in the circle talk about how they are reacting. By the time they receive the eagle feather, many have gone to another level. By the time they receive the drum, they will either sing or pray. Many will have visions.

The talking circle is both a gift from the sweat lodge ceremony and preparation for its greater powers. By sitting in a talking circle and reclaiming their taste, smell, hearing, touch and sight, many people make themselves receptive to worlds beyond the normal physical senses.

Pipe

Tobacco: friendship, peace

11 / CREATION STORIES FROM THE FOURTH WORLD:

White Buffalo Calf Woman brings the pipe

Stories from the fourth world take the elements of a culture and transform them into a religion, one that formalizes the bond between the people and the creator. At the time these stories originated, the people were continuing to deny the source of their power, the way Stone Boy had. They were fighting among themselves and with other Indian nations. They were both arrogant and fearful.

The person who comes to save the people, the most sacred figure in our mythology, is the White Buffalo Calf Woman, also known as Wohpe. She brings the sacred pipe with instructions for its use. She pulls together the seven sacred rituals and puts them into a hierarchy. She promises to reappear regularly, each time bringing a gift.

The stories reflect an increasingly settled people who were developing agriculture and building a civilization.

Early one morning before sunrise, two men were standing on a hill looking around to see where the animals had made a path to water. In the distance, they saw someone coming toward them. It was an Indian woman bent under the weight of a huge bundle tied on her back. She was dressed in white buckskin. She had black braids to her knees. She was very beautiful.

The younger man immediately had evil thoughts and told the older man of his intentions.

"You must not have such bad thoughts," warned the older man. "Surely this woman is *wakan* (holy) and sent by Mapiyato."

The woman approached the men and put down her bundle. She motioned for the younger man to come close to her. When he was next to her, a cloud enveloped them. When the cloud lifted, the woman was alone. At her feet was a pile of bleached bones. Snakes crawled on the younger man's skull.

"I am coming to speak to your people," the woman told the remaining man. "I wish to speak to Hehlokecha Najin."

The man listened but was afraid to look at her. He kept his head bowed.

"You must return and tell your leader to prepare a place for my bundle," the woman instructed him.

He rushed back to his camp and told everyone what he had seen. The whole camp began to prepare for the woman's visit. The people set up a medicine tipi, with twenty-eight poles. When the woman arrived, she went inside, unwrapped her bundle and took out a pipe and a stone. Then she walked in the direction of the sun's arc and stood in front of Hehlokecha Najin. She bowed her head and gave him the red pipe.

"With this you will, during the winters to come, send your voice to Wakan Tanka," she told him. "The bowl of this pipe is the mother earth. The bison calf carved on the bowl is the four ages. The stem of the pipe is all that grows on the earth. The twelve eagle feathers that hang from the stem are from the Wanbli Galeshka, the spotted eagle. All things of the universe are joined to you who smoke the sacred pipe and send your voices to the great Wakan Tanka."

Next, the woman showed the people the seven circles. She carried a stone with seven circles, each smaller than the last, etched into it.

"These seven circles which you see on this stone have much meaning, for they represent the seven rituals in which the red pipe will be used forever."

The woman stayed in the camp and instructed the people in the seven rituals. As she was leaving, she promised to come back again and to bring another gift each time she returned. She walked away in the direction from which she had come. Soon she began to roll. The people watched as she was transformed first into a black buffalo calf, then into a red calf, then yellow, and finally into a glowing white buffalo calf.

The badger began the work of digging toward the light. It was too strong for his sensitive eyes. The mole dug farther but soon was blinded, too. The gray mouse took over and made the final breakthrough. The light, when it hit him full in the face, was so strong that it sheared off his long snout and he became short-nosed.

Corn Woman, who had been sent underground by Wakinyan, thrust her head into the sunlight and shaded her eyes. The surface was still packed hard around her.

Wakinyan, the thunder, roared in the east and shook the earth loose so that Corn Woman and all the underground animals came to the surface.

Corn Woman visited a man who lived alone in the forest. She rubbed against the man's feet and awakened him.

"This must be a spirit," he said.

"I have come to invite you to my house," Corn Woman said.

"I will come," said the man, and he rose and followed her.

Then she disappeared, leaving him crying: "Whoever you are, wherever you are, wait for me. I don't know how to find your house."

When Corn Woman did not respond, he went home and went back to sleep.

She came to him again and asked him to follow. And when he did, she disappeared again.

So he cut a hole in his tipi big enough for an arrow to pass through, and he stood back, waiting for Corn Woman.

She did come again, and before she could lure him away, he let his arrow fly. He heard it strike something that sounded like a sack of pebbles.

When he went out to see what he had hit, he found corn heaped on the ground. He saw that some of the kernels had scattered and appeared to form a path into the forest.

The man followed the path. The trail of corn ended at a circle. When the man dug into the circle, he found a bag of dried meat, a bag of dried turnips, a bag of dried cherries and, at last, a bag of corn, with his arrow still in it.

The old man had found a cache, a hiding place for

dried food. Soon after this, the people performed the first *hunka* ceremony, the making of relatives.

Corn Woman traveled westward while kingfisher pointed the way. Owl led them through dark forests, and loon led them across all the rivers.

Corn Woman found the people living in the Paha Sapa, and she taught them to play shinny and to plant maize. She told them stories about the Star Council.

One day Corn Woman returned to her home in the sky.

Left to themselves, the people began to quarrel and to argue about the games and how the corn was to be cared for. They killed each other.

One day a man appeared. His hair was beautiful and hung down to his waist. He carried a staff hung with scalps.

He was Nesaru, an Arikara from the north. He advised the people to live in peace and have a leader. He gave them rules of honor, which included the taking of a lock of hair from the enemy to gain his bravery and to release his soul.

Taopi Gli and a friend went deer hunting near a cave, now called Wind Cave. They made their kill and were cutting the meat when Taopi Gli caught sight of a woman. He walked to where she had appeared.

Taopi Gli followed her into the cave and sat with her. She wore a headband of intricately designed colors adorned with eagle plumes.

Taopi Gli's friend watched him and the woman in the cave. When she realized that she was being stared at, the woman got up and withdrew deeper into the cave. Taopi Gli got up and followed. His friend tried to shout a warning to prevent him from being hypnotized and lured away. No words came from his parched throat. A hissing sound came from the cave, and Taopi Gli and the woman were gone.

Taopi Gli's friend searched everywhere for him. When he did not find him, the whole camp went into mourning.

Taopi Gli was not dead. He had gone to visit the Tatanka, the Buffalo People, the Maka Mahe Oyate. Because of his visit, famine was no longer known among his people. He had opened the *tatiopi* (way) to the world below. When he returned to his people, herds of buffalo and other game followed him. The buffaloes' sharp hooves cut through a high ridge following him. The people call that cut Buffalo Gap.

Many, many years ago there was a great drought. The people were starving. A huge snake came and swallowed all the water in the ponds, streams, lakes, rivers and oceans.

Remembering the words of the White Buffalo Calf Woman, the people made pipes from the red pipestone and made a small buffalo for the stem and drew designs of the spider on it. The Ocheti Shakowin Oyate prayed with their pipes, while several of the men went west to hunt.

The children suddenly came running, calling out for all the people to come and look at the returning warriors. They were riding on huge sea turtles, crawling over the prairies. The people rejoiced that they would have food.

Once a young man did not have enough presents to give the pretty maiden's parents, so the two lovers ran away and lived along the pathway to the Mountains of the Serpents, the Rocky Mountains. They kept moving, following the seasons.

The next summer, the young man returned to the place where he and the maid had first made love. There he found a pretty flower with scented leaves. He took the plant home and showed it to the elders.

"When it is dried, we will smoke it," said the men. "And we will name it 'where we come together again.' " They chose that name because the man and woman had been so at peace.

Once dried, the tobacco was given to the parents of the girl, and everyone was at peace. Thereafter, tobacco was smoked at every council to promote peace and friendship among tribes.

Three Oglala warriors went out to hunt buffalo. Two of them each killed a deer. The third one could find nothing at all to kill. He was so ashamed that he did not want to return to camp with the others. He stayed alone and fell asleep in some bushes.

During the night, dew drops fell in a spider web above him. When he awakened, the sun in the drops cast colors, spots, arcs and rings of light in elaborate geometric patterns.

This is where he learned the pattern that became the design of all the Oglala Oyate.

The diamond is the symbol for the eyes of Wakan Tanka. The cross in the center of the diamond stands for the four directions. The two triangles attached to the

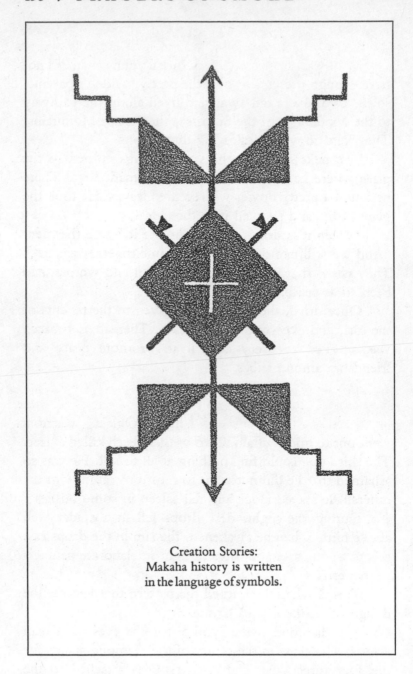

Creation Stories:
Makaha history is written
in the language of symbols.

diamond symbolize the sky. The four streaks of lightning represent the powers of Wakan Tanka. The two arrows represent spiritual food.

In the early days of Indian life, large animals were scarce and travel was slow. The people were often tired and hungry from going long distances on foot.

Several Oglala men were wading through deep snowdrifts one day when they were startled to see, among the trees, a beautiful woman. She wore white buckskin. In her right hand she held a pipe made from bone and decorated with feathers.

She offered the men the pipe and instructed them to take it back to their people. She told them to travel south at the next sunrise.

The warriors did as she said. They found creatures that looked like large dogs. They named them *sunkawakan*, meaning sacred dog. They learned that these strong creatures would carry them or their burdens on their backs. The warriors had been given horses.

During the lifetime of Hehlokecha Najin, the ritual of the keeping of souls developed. Hehlokecha Najin's son had died. Hehlokecha Najin took a lock of hair from his boy's forehead and put it in a soul-keeping bundle for a year. After one year, he burned the hair, and his son's soul was released.

Hehlokecha Najin was an old man when he passed the pipe on to Nunpa Iyanka, who received the sacred pipe with humility. Holding the bowl in his right hand and pointing the stem up toward Wakan Tanka, he gave a prayer in honor of the four directions. He filled the pipe, letting the smoke drift. Turning to the east, he prayed. Then he turned and prayed to the south, the west and the north.

"This is the ritual that will be used by all my people until the ends of their lives," he said.

Before long, the time came for the White Buffalo Calf Woman to reappear. Each time that she had come, she had brought a gift for the people. They were eager for her return.

She touched the earth and from that place the spirit powers grew. The people caught them and put them into bundles. A new ritual had begun. It was called *wakan kitchewa*, meaning "the friendly society of the spirits." The holy man always spoke to the spirits before throwing a new pipe bag to its new owner.

After many years, the Oglala Oyate understood all the rituals of both the stone and bone pipes. They held special ceremonies in the passing on of both pipes. They had feasts and dances.

It was after one of these dances that a young man, Hehlocha Najin, told a story about how he had talked with the Buffalo Calf Woman known as Wohpe. He said she had shown him where to find kinnikinnick, the red willow bark. She had advised him to mix tobacco with the bark.

After Nunpa Iyanka, the pipe was passed to Bad Warrior in 1758; to Elk Head, around 1834; to Martha Bad Warrior, in 1897. All have been members of the Minneconjou band of the Sioux tribes. Today the pipe carrier is Looking Horse.

Keeping of the Soul

Cedar: cleansing, healing
Symbol of uniting
the human people
and the spirit people

Friendship: making
of relatives (*Hunka*)

12 / THE FOURTH WORLD INTERPRETED:

The last two great rituals link humanity and send the soul home

When I was growing up, the story of Wohpe's coming to lead the people back to Wakan Tanka thrilled me no matter how often I heard it. In one version of the Wohpe story, lightning splits the sky and she emerges, shining, from the slit. I always visualized her as a glowing presence, sometimes a woman almost too beautiful to look at, sometimes a white buffalo calf, that most sacred and rare creature.

As an adult, I discovered the celestial event that gave Wohpe her radiance. My research for this book led me to the papers of George Sword, who was an elder of the Smoke People, a sub-band of the Oglala. In the late 1880s, Sword wrote that White Buffalo Calf Woman's name *Wohpe* meant "comet".

Sword's translation of the name made sense to me. A comet would certainly have gotten people's attention and reminded them of the powers of the Great Mystery. And Sword was not the only nineteenth-century Sioux who left a written account of the coming of Wohpe. The other was Battiste Good, who was a Hunkpapa, a member of that band of Sioux designated to serve as gatekeepers whenever the entire nation camped at Buffalo Gap. Both Good's and Sword's accounts of Wohpe were preserved by what was then known as the Bureau of Ethnology.

Good claimed that Wohpe first appeared around 930 A.D. and that she reappeared approximately every seventy years. I believe this means that Wohpe is Halley's Comet, which is known to have appeared in 1531, 1607, 1682, 1758, 1834, 1910 and 1986. Modern science tells us that Halley's Comet comes into our range of vision approximately every seventy-six years.

Good's information that Wohpe appeared in 930 came to him in a vision. He was a great seer. He described another of his visions this way:

In the year of 1856, I went to the Black Hills and cried, and cried, and cried, and suddenly I saw a bird above me, which said: "Stop crying; I am a woman, but I will tell you something: My Great-Father, Father God, who made this place, gave it to me for a home and told me to watch over it. He put a blue sky over my head and gave me a blue flag to have with this beautiful green country. My Great-Father, Father God, grew, and his flesh was part earth and part stone and part metal and part wood and part water; he took from them all and placed them here for me, and told me to watch over them. I am the Eagle-Woman who tells you this. The whites know that there are four black flags of God; that is, four divisions of the earth. He first made the earth soft by wetting it, then cut it into four parts, one of which, containing the Black Hills, he gave to the Dakotas, and, because I am a woman, I shall not consent to the pouring of blood on this dwelling place, i.e., the Black Hills. The time will come that you will remember my words, for after many years you shall grow up one with the white people." She then circled round and round and gradually passed out of my sight. I also saw prints of a man's hands and horses' hooves on the rocks, and two thousand years, and one hundred millions of dollars. I came away crying, as I had gone.

In this vision, Good anticipated the Sioux's loss of their land and the inadequate compensation they were later offered for it.

Another part of the Wohpe story is that she will return twenty-eight times. By my calculations, she has made fifteen of her allotted appearances. I do not know what will happen when she comes for the last time, and neither do I know what gift she brought us when she blazed across the sky in 1986.

Her first appearance is what concerns me, for that is when my people learned the significance of the pipe.

The bowl of the pipe is a circle encompassing every earthbound hope. We touch fire, the eternal love of the Great Spirit, to the bowl's contents; the smoke carries our hopes to the source of their realization. The twelve feathers from the spotted eagle, which hang where the bowl joins the stem, are for vision, for the soaring spirit of the people.

We believe that the original red pipe, the one Wohpe took out of her bundle and gave to Hehlokecha Najin, is still in our possession. Looking Horse is entrusted with its care. He lives in Green Grass, South Dakota, and there, once a year, he holds a ceremony for the viewing of the pipe. After a solemn procession, he takes out the bundle and unwraps it. Everyone who wishes can take a turn looking at the pipe. It is not smoked any more or even touched.

When Martha Bad Warrior, who died in 1936 at age 101, was guardian of the pipe, she used it in ceremonies.

The bone pipe, which Wohpe brought on a subsequent visit, has become the kind of pipe that people use in their personal rituals. Pipestone pipes are scarce and usually saved for ceremonies.

Bone pipes are made from deer or elk antlers. People form the pipe from the elbow of an antler. One end is the bowl and the other is for inserting the wooden stem.

Elk pipe smokers have their own society, which is believed to have extraordinary powers in affairs of the heart. When my grandfather Theodore Means was young and single and trying to get a certain woman to acknowledge him, he went to his medicine man, who was named Looks Twice, and asked him for a love potion. Looks Twice had the power of the elk. He mixed herbs, powdered elk bone and the crushed, dried eye of an elk for my grandfather.

My grandfather carried this mixture with him whenever he went to a feast. If the woman he desired was there, he discreetly put a bit of the mixture into her food. He kept this up, and one day he finally got to talk to her.

She was engaged to be married, but she said he could approach her and talk to her whenever he liked. He and his love potion kept after her for about three years. He had to go back to Looks Twice several times for refills.

Looks Twice gave him a different kind of medicine for discouraging the man to whom she was engaged. This was straight elk bone powder. Whenever my grandfather was near the other man, he put the powder on the palm of his hand and blew it toward his rival. My grandfather was discreet about this, too. The other man never knew he was the target of elk dust.

Finally, the woman's resistance was gone, and she agreed to marry my grandfather. They lived together until he died. She is Theresa Means, my grandmother. She never remarried, although he died twenty-five years ago and she has had many suitors since.

My grandmother loves to tell the Wohpe stories. She has been my main source of information. She is now the eldest Makaha in Wounded Knee, and she is a link to the old ways.

Wohpe's gift to the people on another visit was the ritual of the friendly society of the spirits. The purpose of this ceremony is to gain power from the spirit of animals or something else in nature.

A medicine man makes a spirit bag out of buckskin. It's a small pouch, about two inches long with a leather string attached to it. Once the power is in there, you wear the pouch around your neck for strength and protection.

The medicine man captures the spirit that is appropriate to each individual. He prays and asks for a vision.

Before Melvin did his first sun dance, he asked for a spirit bag. His pouch has tobacco, sage, sweet grass and a crystal in it.

When he had his accident, his spirit bag disappeared. It was the first thing that I checked for at the hospital after going in to see Melvin. He wore that little pouch all the time. But when I asked where his things were, I found only his clothes. Nobody knew anything about his spirit bag.

At home, we looked for the pouch. Finally, in one of my suitcases, where I had some eagle feathers, I found his little spirit pouch. It probably returned there right after the accident. Once I found it, I would take it to the hospital and hold it in his hand while I talked to him.

A spirit bag is essential for anyone who wants to participate in any of the main rituals. Often people go into a sweat lodge without the protection of a spirit bag. I've seen so many of them panic and leave. A spirit bag provides strength to cope with all the power that comes together in a sweat lodge.

Besides describing Wohpe's visits and gifts, the stories from the fourth world bring us the last two great rituals, which could come only after people became more settled. Corn Woman seems to be Wohpe's contemporary. The first Corn Woman story is about learning to cultivate maize. The thunder god offers Corn Woman to the people, but she is unreliable until one elder finally figures out how to plant her.

Stories from other bands of the Oglala credit the Arikara or Ree with being the first to cultivate corn. Black Elk, in *The Sacred Pipe*, attributes the *hunka*, or making of relatives, ceremony to an encounter between the Ree and the Sioux. The Sioux took the corn that the Ree held sacred, and when the Ree petitioned for its return, a wise Sioux leader united the nations through the making of relatives ceremony. The leader, whose name was Matohoshila, had a vision in which he used the Ree's corn to bring the two tribes together. He believed that the purpose of the ceremony was for the Sioux, who had a direct relationship with the creator, to extend that relationship to other tribes.

The original making of relatives ceremony was four days long. The Oglala offered the Ree a dried buffalo bladder on the first day. On the second day, the Sioux leader offered the Ree leader the pipe. The Ree leader then returned the buffalo bladder, indicating that he wished peace and a relationship with the Sioux. The third day, the two tribes gathered in a twenty-eight-pole lodge. Placed at the altar were dried buffalo meat, the sacred food of the Sioux, and an ear of Ree corn, with a stick pushed into one end and an eagle plume tied to the other end. The eagle plume represented the tassel, the first part of the corn to receive light (the power of the Great Spirit). The stick represented the tree of life. The kernels represented the peoples and all other fruit of the universe.

The Ree then pretended to be on the warpath and scouting for the enemy Sioux. Each Ree warrior carried an ear of corn in his right hand and a corn stalk in his left hand. The warriors waved the cornstalks back and forth and chanted. The motion represented the breath of the Great Spirit.

When the Ree captured the Sioux, they led their captives in a solemn procession to the sacred lodge. They waved the cornstalks as they walked, and they stopped the procession four times in order to howl like coyotes, celebrating their success as warriors.

At the lodge, the Ree gave their Sioux captives gifts and painted their faces, drawing a blue circle around the whole face and blue lines on the forehead, both cheeks and chin. The Ree attached the eagle plumes from their corn to the Sioux heads. Thus decorated, the Sioux were reborn and were one with the Ree.

As a final act symbolic of their union, the Ree chief placed sacred buffalo meat in the mouth of the Sioux chief and declared himself Matohoshila's son. After Matohoshila did the same to the Ree chief, everyone smoked the sacred pipe and the ritual was over.

Black Elk ended his description of this first making of relatives ceremony by saying:

> I wish to mention here, that through these rites a three-fold peace was established. The first peace, which is the most important, is that which comes within the souls of men when they realize their relationship, their oneness,

with the universe and all its Powers, and when they realize that at the center of the universe dwells Wakan Tanka, and that this center is really everywhere, it is within each of us. This is the real Peace, and the others are but reflections of this. The second peace is that which is made between two individuals, and the third is that which is made between two nations. But above all you should understand that there can never be peace between nations until there is first known that true peace which, as I have often said, is within the souls of men.

To this day, we use corn as a symbol of the relationship between two people. The making of relatives ceremony, however, has become associated primarily with weddings. This is one of the seven sacred rituals that was severely diluted when Congress passed a law in 1871 prohibiting the Indians from practicing any of their rituals. The making of relatives ceremony was easily assimilated into Christian ritual.

When a man and woman get married, the parents of the bride usually adopt the groom as a relative. They offer him gifts. Then his parents offer the bride gifts. And the families offer gifts to each other.

The making of relatives ceremony has survived as a more personal ritual than the rest. If you want to make someone a sister or brother, you have a big feast in honor of the person, and you present gifts to all the guests you invite to the feast.

When I was in high school, I made a close friend a sister by taking all our friends out to dinner and giving them all gifts in her honor. To this day we are sisters. When something happens in my family or her family, we help each other. A tie made this way is stronger sometimes than one with your blood relatives.

George Armstrong Custer had a Cheyenne wife who

bore him a son named Yellow Bird. After Custer was killed at Little Bighorn, his wife and child lived among the Smoke People at Pine Ridge. The Smoke People made Yellow Bird a relative. Therefore, when the Smoke People were allotted land, Yellow Bird received his portion, too.

Little Wound, leader of the Bear People, led an attack on a wagon train outside of Scotts Bluff, Nebraska. The warriors killed all the travelers, or so they thought. Just as they were riding off, however, a little boy about nine years old appeared. He had been out exploring when the Oglala attacked. He had a bundle with him containing a picture of his mother and father inscribed with his name. He was Alexander Baxter, born to slaves on a Virginia plantation. Little Wound made him a relative, a son. He was given the Indian name Black Leather. He lived among my people until he died, a very old man. He, too, was allotted land when the whites parceled it out.

My grandfather made relatives of everyone, it seemed. Because of this, I had a hard time finding a marriage partner. Relatives made by ceremony are off-limits the way blood relatives are. Now my boys have the same problem. Thanks to their great-grandfather, they are related to most of the young Makaha women. I remind them that the ties are still strong.

The last of the seven sacred rituals is the keeping of the soul. Among some of my people, this is still practiced in the old way. When my husband Russel died, I followed my ancestors' ceremonies as well as I could.

Russ died in Wounded Knee. I called Bill Good Voice Elk to perform the burial ceremonies and to act as keeper of his soul.

Being a soul keeper is a great responsibility. If the duties are not performed correctly, the soul is unable to become one with the Great Spirit and will wander the earth. The soul keeper must not commit any violent acts and is not permitted to use a knife even to cut his meat. He must keep the soul in tranquil surroundings. Harmony must always prevail where the soul awaits release. The soul keeper usually keeps to himself to avoid the possibility of exposing the soul to agitated people. He cannot swear or become angry. He has to keep his voice down so he won't disturb the soul. Whenever he eats, he must put out another plate for the soul. This custodianship usually lasts for a year.

Bill Good Voice Elk is a Sioux elder and a powerful medicine man. I offered him a pipe, and when he took it he accepted my request that he act as keeper of Russ's soul.

The first thing he did was to cut a lock of hair from my husband's forehead. He burned sweet grass to purify the hair. Then he wrapped it in a buckskin bundle and got ready for the public ceremony.

About fifty relatives and friends gathered in our home in Wounded Knee. Everyone sat on the floor in a darkened room. Bill Good Voice Elk burned sage, sweet grass and cedar and passed the soul bundle over the smoke. My husband's drum was hanging on the wall. We all saw points of light like fireflies dancing over the drum. With each twinkling came a beat. These were Bill Good Voice Elk's helpers. They drummed throughout the ceremony.

My sons and I had prepared tobacco ties, four hundred different-colored ones, as offerings. We presented them. We heard a banging of the screen door, as if as strong wind were battering the house. Bill told us that other souls were coming into the room. It is common for recently departed souls to come back to support someone else who is just entering their realm.

In the talking circle, everyone had a turn verbalizing his or her grief. Everyone asked the purified soul for help in coping with the loss. When the talking was finished, we passed my husband's pipe. The lights came on, and that was the end of the first ceremony.

Because we believe that the spirit does not leave the body for four days, we did not bury my husband until the fifth day after his death. We kept his body in a tipi. We fed scores of people as they came to pay their respects.

My ancestors would take the body to a hilltop and put it on a scaffold made of four trees holding a platform of limbs. They believed that the spirit of the tree remained with the body until it returned to the elements of its forebears, the stars. Later the bones of the departed were buried, and a small cedar tree was planted over the grave. The bones fertilized the spot, and the tree and a new life grew.

We took my husband's body to a burial ground at Wounded Knee. After we buried him, members of the family took turns sitting at his grave for four more days and nights.

These eight days immediately after a person's death are the time for his loved ones to express all their grief. Crying is encouraged. Once the eight days are over, however, the loved ones are to put their grief behind them and not to think of it at all. That is difficult.

After the vigil at the grave, I went through the house and packed all my husband's belongings and took them to the country and burned them. We believe that when a person touches something, his soul leaves a print. These prints can contain hostile or bad feelings and can transmit them to someone else. My husband's soul bothered us until we burned all his things.

A long time ago, even the houses of the dead were

cleansed with smoke and given away. That's what we did when my grandfather died—we saged down his house and gave it away. The soul's prints are very strong.

Bill Good Voice Elk took the bundle with my husband's soul to his house. He treated it with great respect. Whenever he performed a ceremony, he took the bundle with him so that people could pray for the soul to continue on its journey. On sunny days, he took the bundle outside and hung it on a tripod. He made sure that the bundle, which was the size of a softball, faced south, the direction in which the soul travels. The legs of the tripod are at the other three directions. People pay their respects to the soul by placing food offerings at the base of the tripod.

After a year, Bill Good Voice Elk told us to prepare the memorial dinner at which he would release my husband's soul.

During our year of mourning, we had worn black and worked on making the gifts we would offer at the releasing of the soul ceremony. My youngest sister and I had sewed for a couple of hours every night, making twenty-six star quilts, fifteen shawls and thirty embroidered pillows

I was exhausted after that year of mourning. When I heard my husband's drumming in the sweat lodge, I felt as though he appreciated my efforts. I was ready to let him go.

Often, during this final ceremony, the grave and tombstone are covered with a quilt or blanket, which goes afterward to the man who has kept the soul.

For the releasing of the soul, friends and relatives sit outside in a circle. All the food that is to be eaten and the gifts to be given are in the center of the circle. We burn smoke over everything to purify it.

One of my relatives had kept a list of all the people

who stayed for four days and four nights during the funeral and of what they brought during that time. These are the people who receive gifts first. The dead person's family is obligated to give something to anyone who attended the funeral. You do not necessarily have to make all the gifts you offer. You can buy them. They are usually household items. Pendleton blankets are a popular giveaway.

Bill Good Voice Elk prayed for the journey of my husband's soul. He led the singing of my husband's honor song. A relative offered the soul its last meal. At this point my husband was represented by a stick figure with an eagle plume tied to the top. My ancestors used a more elaborate representative called the soul post. This was a willow post with a circle of buckskin painted to look like a face tied to the top and a war bonnet placed over that. They draped a buffalo robe around the willow and put all the deceased's possessions nearby.

After the soul's final meal, Bill Good Voice Elk opened the bundle and burned the lock of hair. He saved the ashes to carry to the grave. Along with the ashes, I buried my wedding rings. We laid the stick figure with the eagle plume atop the grave. My husband's soul was free.

Creator (*Wakan Tanka*
or *Tunkasila*)

Cycles, 4 Ages:
Infancy, Youth,
Middle Age, Old Age

13 / THE WORLD'S SPIRITUAL LANDSCAPE:

Makaha traditions can nourish it

People often ask me if I believe we are living in the last days of the fourth world, when the buffalo has lost nearly all its hair and is wobbling on its last leg. When I answer yes, they want to know why I bother trying to keep my traditions alive. Won't they all be gone soon anyway, when the buffalo finally collapses and our world ends?

Because I have seen how the creation stories reflect celestial events or powerful natural phenomena like floods, volcanos and glaciers, and because I believe that the natural world moves to its own rhythms regardless of human wishes, I have no doubt that the physical world we inhabit will one day be gone or so radically altered that human life will be impossible.

But I have no idea when that will happen. It could be millions of years from now.

And I've been taught that we come from the stars and we will go back to the stars, and we can choose to share in the Great Mystery while we are on this particular planet. I believe our time here will be easier if we make that choice.

I have said that I am eager for my four sons to keep the ways of their ancestors. I want them to do so for two reasons: so that those sacred old ways will nourish a new generation and so that my sons will become whole.

They are good boys and they try to practice the rituals, but the dominant white society discourages them. They are accused of practicing witchcraft because they seek the healing energy of the sweat lodge.

My oldest son Theodore is having the hardest time reconciling his heritage with his life in white America.

He had his first visions when he was only twelve. He told me that every morning around 3:30 an elderly man came to his room. At first I thought he was just having nightmares. Then I stayed with him one night to see for myself.

I set the alarm clock for 3:00 so that we would both be wide awake by 3:30. Theodore told me that he would see a table in the corner and an Indian man sitting at it. The man would get up from the table and beckon to Theodore to follow him. Theodore would follow as far as the window, which presented no obstacle to the man even though it was closed.

At 3:30, we were sitting up when I felt Theodore turn to his right. He said, "Mom, he's here again."

I couldn't see anything, but I watched Theodore go into an altered state. His eyes rolled back in his head, and he started making gurgling sounds. I grabbed him and held him on my lap and kept calling to him, "Come back."

Then I said to the man, "Whoever you are and whatever you want—he's only a little boy and he doesn't understand, so please leave him alone." I burned sage and sweet grass.

When we were next in Wounded Knee, I asked Bill Good Voice Elk to do a ceremony for Theodore so that he could have some peace. Bill told me that Theodore's nightly visitor was his grandfather on his father's side, a man called Black Bird. During the ceremony, Black Bird promised to stop trying to lure Theodore away.

As we were leaving the ceremony, my sister-in-law saw Theodore with hair down to his waist, braided on the left and hanging loose on the right. His left eye had a black line painted over it, running from his nose to his temple.

We asked Bill to do another ceremony to interpret this vision. He told us the way Theodore appeared to my sister-in-law is the way he is to look when he sun dances.

Having visions can be frightening for a child, I know. But I think a culture that acknowledges those visions and shows the child the power to control them is infinitely richer than one that refuses to admit they exist.

When Theodore was fourteen, he had another vision. This time he said that whenever he turned the light off in his room, eagles flew in. He could hear their wings. Again, I sat in his room all night to reassure him. And I asked the medicine man Kenny Moses, of the Sauk Suiattle tribe, to do a ceremony.

Kenny told us that during the ceremony he saw Theodore's ancestors dangling a rope just out of Theodore's reach. Kenny asked what a rope symbolized to the Makaha. I told him that the only time we use a rope is in the sun dance. In that case, he said, Theodore's ancestors must be telling him he is not quite ready for the sun dance.

The sun dance demands courage and strength, but it

returns them doubled. It gives the dancer a union with the Great Mystery that will shape his entire life. It gives him a vision that he can pass on to his children.

When Theodore was sixteen, I began to ask him to consider doing his sun dance. Now he's twenty-four. I am still reminding him of the rewards of the ritual, and he's still telling me that he's not ready.

Once he explained to me that he felt too distracted to make the commitment the sun dance requires. He said that a long time ago, when people had wilderness around them and could go into the mountains without worrying for their safety, they could calm themselves enough to invite their visions. But here in this environment he couldn't find the peace he needed.

At another point, he began to doubt that anyone had spiritual power. He said that so many people were presenting themselves as healers who didn't know the first thing about healing. He thought the only power they wanted was control over other people. He refused to be anyone's pawn.

Last year, when Melvin was in his coma and Kenny Moses was in the hospital room working with him, Theodore stood by his brother's bed. After the ceremony, Kenny told Theodore that he had seen the rope over him again. This time it was within his reach.

Still, Theodore says he's not ready for his sun dance. I tell him that if he waits too long, he will lose the chance to increase his powers. If he lets white society distract him, he will lose his vision.

I try to help him understand how great his loss will be, and how the lives of his two children will be diminished as a result.

When I see Theodore's struggles, I see all the dangers to the continued existence of the Oglala culture. We Oglala were the native peoples who held out the longest against the white invaders. The Sioux were the last Indian nation to be assimilated into white culture. Only one hundred years ago, we were killing and being killed as we battled for our freedom. The Wounded Knee massacre was in December of 1890.

We have lost so much since then. My parents' generation and mine have not done a good job of guarding our heritage. We have let the old ways disappear. Caught in the current of change, all we could do was struggle to survive as everything we knew was swept away.

I was plucked from my grandparents' home at the age of ten and sent away to a school where my classmates shunned me or taunted me as "that little Indian girl." I wanted to get out of my body and into one that had light skin and a turned-up nose.

But I had the stories that my grandparents had given me. As I copied and recopied them, I gained strength even though I didn't understand then where it came from. Eventually I realized that the skin I moved in was something the Great Spirit could touch. No longer did I want to change it. Instead, I wanted to offer it to Wakan Tanka the way others before me had offered the same red skin.

I did not stray too far from the ways of my ancestors. I had grown up hearing the stories and seeing some of the rituals. And my grandparents had instilled in me the reverence for nature that the stories and rituals celebrate.

An Indian person never takes nature for granted. We know that nothing is more important than to acquire the habit of regarding nature and taking strength from it.

We do not need sunsets, mountains, waterfalls or hillsides blanketed with wildflowers before we feel any response to nature. The most common weed or bird can remind us of the way everything on this earth is connected.

The dominant culture apparently does not believe in

the connection of all creation. Otherwise, forests and animals would not be disappearing at such an alarming rate. When I compare the order of things my heritage taught me to the one white society observes, I am appalled.

The Makaha believe that the Great Spirit or Wakan Tanka, which is in all and through all, manifests itself in sixteen powers. They are ranked this way:

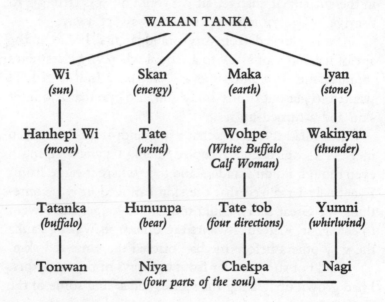

The parts of the soul, which are Wakan Tanka's manifestation in people, are at the bottom of this totem pole. This makes the animals superior to us.

White society has reversed the sixteen powers, putting people on top, and white people at the very top. White people have put themselves above the creator.

If Indian people go along with this upsetting of the order of things, I fear that the end of the fourth world will come unnaturally fast.

My dream is that all people will adopt the Indian point of view; that we will restore the hierarchy of the sixteen powers, with the Great Spirit over all; that we will revere nature and look for guidance there. If we cannot learn from the stones, leaves, grass, streams, birds and animals that share this realm with us, we are lost.

I do not think this is an unrealistic hope. Every day people ask me about the rituals and symbolism of my tribe. These are not just Indian people. They are white people, too, looking for a more reverent way to live. And as I tell the stories and explain the ceremonies, they all find similar myths and rituals from their own heritage.

So it is that one small group of people trying to keep their traditions alive can suggest ways for all people to let the Great Mystery touch them.

GLOSSARY

This listing is divided into two parts: first, the names of characters who appear in the creation stories; second, Olakota terms connected with rituals.

PEOPLE AND GODS IN THE CREATION STORIES

Names of the characters in the creation stories are spelled to reflect the original Olakota dialect in which the stories were told.

From the stories of the first world:

Anpo—dawn and twilight

Chekpa Hoksicalapi—the twins who helped create the first creatures on earth

Ebom—first son of Unktehila and Uncegila

Eya—son of Tate and Ite; originally called Wiyohpeyata, the west wind; his color is black, and the swallow is his messenger

Hanhepi Wi—the moon; she was originally Hanpetu, the spirit of fertility

Hanpetu—the spirit of fertility; she becomes Hanhepi Wi, the moon

Iktome—the Makaha trickster who appears as a spider

Ite—daughter of Wazi and Owankanka, wife of Tate, mother of the four winds; she becomes Anong Ite, the two-faced one, when she betrays her husband and family

Iya—second son of Unktehila and Uncegila

Iyan—Grandfather Stone, the one who names things; also called Tunka

Ksa—the spider spirit of wisdom and language; he becomes Iktome when he loses favor with the other spirits

Ksapela—third son of Unktehila and Uncegila

Maka—the earth

Mapiyato—spirit of the sky

Mini Watutkala—fourth son of Unktehila and Uncegila

Okaga—son of Tate and Ite; originally called Ito Kagata, the south wind; his color is yellow and his messenger is the owl

Owankanka—the female bison, wife of the leader of the Bison People

Peta Yuhala—the maker of the fireball that broke to form the universe

Star Council—all the bodies of the universe

Tate—motion

Uncegila—the dinosaur that was the second creature created

Unci—the great-grandmother, who receives the souls of the dead

Unktehila—the water monster that was the first creature created

Wakinyan—the winged spirit of thunder

Wazi—the male bison, leader of the Bison People

Wi—the sun

Yanpa—son of Tate and Ite; originally called Wiyohiyanpata, the east wind; his color is red, and the meadowlark is his messenger

Yata—son of Tate and Ite; originally called Waziyata, the north wind; his color is white, and the magpie is his messenger.

Yumni—the whirlwind, symbol of lovemaking

From the stories of the second world:

Anpa Wicahpi—a young Peta Oyate woman who falls in love with snake-man, Wicasa Hanska

Chekpa Oyate—the Twin People waiting at Bear Butte, South Dakota to be born

Hinhan Hota—a Peta Oyate warrior who destroys the offspring of Anpa Wicahpi and snake-man

Inawizi—the first woman to live on earth

Iyapa—the camp crier who starts the bloody race among all creatures on earth

Ocheti Shakowin—the Seven Campfires or tribes of the Sioux nation, comprising the Oglala (Scattering of Ashes), Itazipcho (Without Bows), Minneconjou (Plant Beside the Stream), Sihasapa (Black Feet), Sichangu (Burned Thighs), Hunkpapa (At the Camping Circle Entrance) and Ooenunpa (Two Boiling Kettles)

Oyate Teztela—the Little People, helpers of the Oglala

Peta Oyate—the Fire People; the first name given to the Oglala

Tiatuwan Oyate—People Lost and Looking for a Home; the third name given to the Oglala

Tokahe—the first man to live on earth

Wazia Wichaghpi Owanjihan—the leader of the North Star nation; his meanness drives the Big Dipper nations out of the sky and onto earth

Wicasa Hanska—snake-man

Zuzeca Oyate—the Snake People; the second name given to the Oglala

From the stories of the third world:

Chaske—oldest uncle of Stone Boy

Hepan—second oldest uncle of Stone Boy

Star-man—Venus; his wife is Mars, and his son is Mercury

Stone Boy—the first human to have healing powers; discoverer of the sweat lodge

Tunkasila—maker of the first pipe

Wi Tokape—mother of Stone Boy

From the stories of the fourth world:

Corn Woman—the figure sent by Wakinyan to give people agriculture

Hehlocha Najin—the Sioux discoverer of kinnikinnick

Hehlokecha Najin—leader of the Sioux when White Buffalo Calf Woman appears the first time and thus the first keeper of the pipe

Nesaru—the Arikara warrior who teaches the removal of the enemy's hair to gain his power and release his soul

Nunpa Iyanka—the Sioux leader who taught people to pray with the pipe to the four directions

Taopi Gli—the man who brings the buffalo to the people

Tatanka—Buffalo People; also known as Maka Mahe Oyate

White Buffalo Calf Woman—the most sacred figure in the Sioux tradition, who comes to show people the way back to Wakan Tanka, the creator; she brings the sacred pipe and instructions for its use; she is known also as Wohpe, which is translated as "comet"

MAKAHA RITUAL TERMS

hanblecheyapi—vision seeking, one of the seven great rituals

heyoka—the thunder ritual, in which everything is done backwards

hunka—the making of relatives, one of the seven great rituals

hunkapi—a series of ceremonies that prepare a girl for her first menstruation

inipi—the sweat lodge, one of the seven great rituals

ishna ta awi cha lowan—preparing a girl for womanhood, one of the seven great rituals

kumugha—ceremony in which the hair of a menstruating woman brings a disrespectful man to his knees

sicun—soul; the four parts of sicun are *tonwan* (eye), *niya* (breath), *chekpa* (animal spirit twin) and *nagi* (guardian)

tapa wanka yap—the throwing of the ball, one of the seven great rituals

wacanga—sweet grass, used for purification in all rituals

wakan kitchewa—the friendly society of the spirits, a ritual for the capture of spirit powers

Wakan Tanka—the creator of all things

wiwanyag wachipi—the sun dance, one of the seven great rituals

INDEX